Help Me Be a Good Girl Amen

My Journey from
Missionary Kid to Truth

Rebecca Jean Terry

"You have saved the best till now."
[John 2:10]

The cover picture was taken in 1929.
A friendly rickshaw man brought me home
when he found me wandering
outside the mission compound.

Bible quotations are
from various translations

Some of my watercolors are added

Copyright 2011 Rebecca Jean Terry

Library of Congress
United States Copyright
#TXu-742-845
January 13, 2011

Brandy Wine Press

2347 Birch Bay Lynden Road
Custer, WA 98240
360-366-4124
brandywinepress@comcast.net

This story is dedicated to:

My two sons
My four daughters
My ten granddaughters
My eleven grandsons
My twenty-one great grandchildren
All their spouses
All future arrivals
Christ for the Nations, Canada
My friends around the world
And to all those folks who told me
"You should write a book!"

Rebecca Jean Terry

And special thanks to
Grace who patiently helped
me through editing and countless bouts
of computer-itis!

CONTENTS

PART ONE: BE A GOOD GIRL AMEN 7

Be A Good Girl, Amen 8
The Secret at South Gate..9
Evacuation Trails and Trials 11
Out to India 16
Getting to the States 16
The Ship Trips 24
Putting it Together 34
Culture Shock 39
The Folks' Place 45

PART TWO: THE FAMILY 51

Learning about Sex 52
The Double Date 54
Naming Kids 55
The Champ 59
I Can Believe!...59

PART THREE: THE HOUSE ON THE SAND 63

Projects, Ahoy! 64
The Wilderness 75
Nora and John 79
Living with Insanity 85
Amazing Love 86

My fault too 87
The Rose Bush is Gone... 88

PART FOUR: PRESSING ON 91

Wells Fargo Recovery 92
General's dog dish 93
Precious in the Sight of the Lord................................. 96
The Ex- Police Officer 100

PART FIVE: STARTING OVER 103

Whatcom Pregnancy Center 105
Christ for the Nations...106
Free Indeed 107
Smuggling Bibles..109
Return to Route Winling...114
Standing beside myself: 120
The Dream 121

PART ONE
Be a Good Girl Amen

When I was a child, I spoke as a child, I understood as a child, I thought as a child; but when I became a man, I put away childish things. For now we see in a mirror, dimly but then face to face. Now I know in part, but then I shall know just as I also am known.

[1 Corinthians 13:11-12]

Becky Jean, Age 5, 1932

{Born in China, June 27, 1926}

Be A Good Girl Amen

As long as I can remember I always prayed before I went to sleep – as fast as I could:
"God bless Mother and Daddy, Grandma,
Aunt T, Uncle Percy, Danny, Warny, Dicky,
and help me to be a good girl Amen."

Then I'd bury myself under the covers and go to sleep. That's because being a good girl had been my primary goal in life ever since the BIG SPANKING Daddy gave me when I was five, after he found the boy paper dolls I made with "that thing boys have in their fronts." There must be something very naughty about girls because my brothers and the boys next door could run around naked in the water hose on hot days but I had to wear panties.

Being a good girl meant being very good around Daddy, never talking back, always minding, trying to never cry, and doing good things that people would like—but often meant telling little lies to be sure I wouldn't get in trouble over anything.

Being a good girl was so rewarding that I often had a righteous swelling in my chest when I did something Really Good. The year the Japanese attacked Shanghai and burned down the mission compound and we were camped in the boys' dorm of the American School, I did something Really Good. I was sick in bed listening to the radio. Portable radios were scarce in 1937, but I got to have ours in my room because I couldn't go to school.

While I was listening a guy broke in and announced that the Japanese were going to be bombing the city, starting at noon. Everybody should close their stores and schools and head for shelter.

I told my mom and she told the principal and he closed the school and sent the kids home. Boy, did I feel SWELL! I had a swollen chest all the rest of the week that I was the one that closed the school!

Shanghai American School
as it looked from the boys' dorm, 1937

The Secret at South Gate

The Presbyterian mission compound, South Gate, in the Native City of Shanghai, was established in the 1890's. The walled compound consisted mainly of the spacious campus of Mary Farnham School, the first all girls' school in China. A fence separated the school from six massive missionary homes in the rest of the compound, reflecting the Victorian homes popular at that time in cities like New York and San Francisco. They were three story red brick structures with wide verandas, large enough to handle half a dozen mosquito-netted cots when summer got blistering. The Terry family moved into the biggest of these in November, 1934, when I was eight.

What to do with all that room! The halls and staircase were simply huge. I could mount the banister upstairs and slide all the way down around a curve and land with a plop in the front hall. That center hall branched off with a smaller one along side and under the stairs — enough room to store six bicycles. And the summer that Dad bought a row boat for the boys they stored it in the main part of the hall between the living room and dining room doors!

The ceilings were at least ten feet high, and every interior door had a glass transom over it, a window hinged on top with a pulley to pull it open for ventilation. Sometimes Danny and Warny had pillow fights through the transoms. In winter the house was heated by fireplaces, four up, four down, two on each of the four chimneys.

In 1938 when Dad took me with him to see the compound after the Japanese burned everything down, all that was left were piles of white-burned bricks, green globs of melted window glass, and four chimneys towering over the rubble. On one upstairs chimney, way above my head, I spied two little cars on the partly burned mantle. Even at age twelve I appreciated the irony that everything was gone except two abandoned Tootsie toys.

The third floor attic at the top of a smaller staircase was on the other side of a normal door. Light came from a window on one side, but the other side was under the eaves. It was my favorite place to be alone. There were big steamer trunks painted with diagonal yellow lines and plastered with pealing stickers: CANADIAN PACIFIC STEAMSHIP LINES, or AMERICAN DOLLAR LINES. The trunks were full of curious things like Dad's huge scrapbooks of World War I, army boots, flags in tight khaki bags, his Army Air Corps uniform, badges, helmets, and a brass bugle.

Being the snoopy kid I was, I spent hours looking at the pictures of soldiers and battlefields. I hoped to see something Really Gory, but the faded newspaper clippings were disappointingly dull. I was always careful to put things back just the way I found then, and then be about my own business.

The biggest secret of all secrets was that I was a WRITER. Under the eaves, through a half-sized little door, where the roof sloped down and met the attic floor, there was a long tunnel, dark and mysterious. Nobody ever knew I was there! That was where I put a candle on a box, spread out my notebook, closed the door and wrote about the Family with Ten Children.

All the girls had names like Jackie, Jo, Gerry, Bobbie, Sandy: boy's names. My heroine, you see, was Jo in *Little Women*. I was sure I could write a story like that.

It's a good thing I, Becky Jean Terry, the budding author, secretly writing with a candle flickering under the eaves, was not the one responsible for burning the house down!

Dan, Warren, Dick and Becky Jean,
with our kites, at South Gate
Shanghai, 1935

Evacuation Trails and Trials

In 1940 after we had spent a furlough year in Ohio and left Dan and Warren behind in college, the American Consulate ordered Americans to leave China. But Dad was determined to go to West China, also called Free China at the time. The Japanese occupied most of the coast, as well as gradually penetrating through to the western provinces. In preparation for complete occupation, they were consistently bombing the major cities, even as far as Chengdu, where we were going. There was a Canadian School we could attend and Dad planned to some way continue his work for the Christian Literature Society.

There was a big adventure ahead; Dick and I looked forward to the trip, even though we didn't know what lay ahead, and often there were no predictable means of transportation. However, Dad, Mom, Dick and I set out, first by overnight ship north to Tsingtao [now Qingdao] then by train back south to Pengpu ["Bung-pu"], where we were stuck.

And there I got my first period. How to deal with that? Mom bought me a bunch of little towels and showed me how to

11

fold them and pin them on a belt. I hated them! They were a huge nuisance, embarrassing, and smelly. I had to soak them in a bucket of water for the rest of my life, it seemed. We never asked servants to wash them so everywhere we went I washed them myself—most often with no running water—and dried them as inconspicuously as possible, usually on a towel rack under another towel so as not to be visible all over the place. It was one more confirmation that boys had it much better than girls.

By the time we had reached Pengpu our party had swelled to twenty three, including two families with small children and several brand new missionary ladies assigned to the China Inland Mission (CIM). They came from England, Australia, and New Zealand, and were genuinely ready, they told us, to lay down their lives for Jesus regardless of inconveniences and uncertainties ahead.

Nothing happened quickly. A delay could be two or three weeks as the men worked with either Japanese or Chinese authorities, depending on where we were held up. Some days we were intercepted by Chinese in the morning and Japanese in the afternoon -- or vice versa -- as they wondered across no-man's-land. Often these small bands of soldiers were young teenagers, more curious to poke into our baggage than to do anything more aggressive.

Our first delay was about two weeks in an old church with a rickety foot-pumping organ. The CIM ladies sang a lot and prayed fervently every day for a breakthrough which did come in the person of a Japanese official who said he was a Christian. He made the right intercessions for the group to proceed, but there was no transportation except on carts. These were flat bed affairs between two bicycle wheels, drawn by a coolie: sort of a flat rickshaw. We started out with 43 carts, one for each person and the rest for the baggage. The coolies were a cheerful bunch of strong guys, sometimes racing their carts just for the fun of it.

The cart trip ended after a few days when we got to the edge of the Yellow River flood, which covered several hundred square miles.

Flood --another crisis to solve. A lot of bickering and bargaining went on between Dad and some junk [boat] owners before they reached an agreement to let us hire several boats to cross the flood waters. The junk assigned to the "Terriers" was already occupied by a mom, dad, and six kids! They squeezed themselves in somehow and gave us the main "cabin" which was nothing more than a bamboo mat draped over a pole. When I leaned against the side of my "bunk," the mat would push away to expose me to the flood water practically at my elbows.

Once in a while one of the junks would get stuck. The long poles that the boatmen used to push us along might not be long enough to touch the bottom, or in some situations we might be stuck on the roof of a house underwater.

The biggest problem was drinking water. Fortunately our boat family had a little brass kettle with a place for burning charcoal underneath. This they used to boil water for us, but... it was muddy flood water contaminated with goodness knows what. Mother solved the problem by boiling once, pouring out the top, emptying the kettle, boiling a second or third time till all the silt was gone. Then she added Eagle Brand Condensed milk to our cups to disguise the taste.

There was access to dry land here and there, some dykes we could walk on, and some little villages struggling to survive. So we could occasionally stop and get jao-tzes [steamed buns] which were always one of my favorite Chinese foods.

The water trip lasted ten days till we got to a mission station at Loyang. Oh, my! The best most wonderful bath I ever had in my life was waiting for me there. I would have stayed in the tub all day if it hadn't been somebody else's turn after me.

We had dropped off some of the CIM ladies by now and the rest set off from Loyang to their assigned stations. It had gotten to be quite a joke on the cart trip because curious villagers on the way would ask where the rich man with all the wives was going.

I had always dreamed about being a doctor, well maybe I could be a writer and a doctor, so in Loyang I asked the mission doctor if I could observe some operations. He was very gracious to let me into the operating room, which was a simple room with a big window. Not any fancy equipment, just a nurse assisting and me watching. After the first operation, in which he removed a woman's breast, he turned to me and said, "Now I am going to remove a gall bladder." In my innocence, I was so embarrassed by the word *bladder*, I thought he meant I should leave, which I did. Then I wandered around the compound aimlessly the rest of the day, wishing I had stayed.

After recovering for a few days, we were able to reach the next city – by cart or rickshaw, I don't remember. But by now, having visited several mission stations, Dad realized that they all had a serious shortage of Bibles and other literature. He felt so strongly about this that he and Mom agreed that we could go on without him and he would return to Shanghai and smuggle as many Bibles as possible into Free China.

After saying goodbye to Dad, and more delays, Dick and Mom and I were able to get a ride with a mail truck that went from Xian to Chengdu, a trip of several days over three mountain ranges. Mom and I rode in the cab with the driver, and Dick hung to the mail bags in the back along with a few Chinese who also were packed along.

For Dad, this decision ushered in the major accomplishment of his career. During the next two years he managed to get 35 tons of Bibles through the Japanese lines and distribute them to five central provinces. The Christian Literature Society [CLS] had never published Bibles, but had been their main distributor, as they were supplied by the American Bible Society.
When we left Shanghai there were huge stock piles of Bibles waiting to be delivered to the Chinese, but there had been no way because of the Japanese occupation.
Dad discovered a little town on a canal off the river, which had been occupied by the Japanese before the flood. Then after the waters receded, and by some judicious canal digging by the Chinese, the little town was now isolated on the Chinese side of the river, yet with a fully operating Japanese post office!
Dad sent word to Shanghai to start mailing Bibles in small packages of two or three. At first he met with objections, even absolute refusal from the Mission Board who thought the plan was too risky. "Okay," Dad told them, "then I will borrow on my salary and pay for it myself."
The Japanese weren't about to admit the loss of a town, and being famous for their efficiency, they were the ones who ferried the mail across the canal--right in keeping with God's plan!
Dad met the first shipment on the Chinese side and whisked it away on a bicycle, later in ox carts, without a hitch. After the success of the first few capers, the Mission Board caught the vision and backed him up one hundred percent.
There were times when he had to hide, times when he would be met outside a town and be warned by a messenger that his life was at risk if he were caught, but he didn't give up. He set up a re-distribution center in a city that was being regularly bombed.

One day when hearing the warning sirens he headed for the dugout in the yard, but just as he was about to step out the door he heard the bomb shrieking down. He ducked inside just as the door blew off and the bomb made a direct hit on the dugout. Dad carried a piece of shrapnel in his back the rest of his life; doctors said it was safer left there than risking damage to his spine by taking it out.

We had left Shanghai in early November and reached Chengdu in late February, a roundabout trip impossible to figure in miles; four months to get there.

Because of the continual bombing of Chengdu by the Japanese, the Canadian School had moved about 70 miles to Renshow, a small mountain village dominated by an ancient pagoda. An old mission hospital covering several acres of terraced hillside had been converted to a boarding school for about 60 kids, grades one through high school.

Probably one of the carriers from Chengdu had brought news of our coming, because a friendly gathering of kids was waiting for us on the old bridge into town. They were as glad to see us as we were to see then – happy to reach the place we'd looked forward to with great anticipation. We weren't disappointed, either. We adjusted to living with roommates, the small classes; enjoyed the exuberant fun and friendships. Never mind that there was no electricity nor running water, or that paper was so scarce we saved every tiny scrap. We had Saturday night dances to records played on a wind-up Victorla and talked long hours after snuffing out our oil lamps. I fell in love with everything and everybody right away.

Mom stayed with us for the little while as a housemother and piano teacher. She was loved by everybody, but she wished she were with Dad. He came to visit us once at Christmas and again in the summer but was in touch only by letters. Mom's letters to him during that time (those that are saved in the Terry Letters) reflect deep disappointment over their long separation.

I'll never forget the day, December 9th, 1941, when Mom burst into our classroom, her face pale in shock, and told us she had just heard that Japan had attacked Pearl Harbor. No one knew where Pearl Harbor was or how significant the date, December 7,1941, was; we didn't even hear about it till someone had called the one telephone in Renshow and given the word to an official there: America was at war and everything would change -- again.

Not long after that Mom got word that Dad had had a heart attack. He was then in southeast China, north of Hong

Kong, in Hengyang. She made arrangements right away to leave us in school and join him there.

Inflation in China had risen to an almost ridiculous state. Every bank printed its own money which meant no two bills were alike. A cup of oil which would burn for two nights in an oil lamp went up from 40₵ to $40! Canadians and Americans having to exchange their money at the official exchange rate simply couldn't make it stretch to cover the most basic expenses; thereby all the work including the Canadian School had to shut down.

I hosted a sale for the neighbors and sold what was left of our household stuff. The cash result was two bundles of money, 4x4x4 inches square, which I tied around with shoestrings, hung on the handlebars of my bike, and delivered to the mission treasurer: several thousand worthless Chinese dollars.

That left Dick and me each with only a suitcase of worldly goods to face the future.

Out to India

In 1943 with the Canadian School closed and the folks being 1500 miles away, what were Dick and I to do? I would be 17 in June and Dick would be 15 in July. We were not exactly adults, but we were willing to be! Mom and Dad wrote to Dick advising him to go to school in India, along with some of the other Canadian School kids; at least he wouldn't be half way around the world, and there could be a possibility of their being reunited somewhere in China.

I was ready for my senior year and didn't want to go to India. I cabled the folks and asked their permission to go to the States, provided I could figure out how. They cabled back their agreement and gave me names of people that might help. I was thrilled to be GOING TO THE STATES!!!

The first person I contacted was the mission treasurer who gave me two cashier's checks for $500, gold [U.S.] --a lot of money and I was almost scared to handle it!

[The following dated entries are quotes from my diary.]
Diary: June 1, 1943, On the Renshow-Chengdu Road
Thirty-six of us are sitting by the side of the road near the broken bridge. An open commercial truck brought us this far, and the Friends' Ambulance Unit truck was supposed to meet us, but it hasn't showed up yet. Ah me.

I have just been thinking about me: how I happen to be here and where else I would be if I weren't here and what I'd be doing somewhere else. It's a funny collection of circumstances. There we were, living peacefully in Shanghai when the threat of war got so close we had to move out. Then there we were again, behaving quite well in the Canadian School in Renshow, and now inflation's got so bad we're leaving there. Wonder what's going to drive us next time and where.

Wonder where that old truck can be? If it doesn't come pretty soon it won't be able to find us for the crowd. Already the country people are four deep around our little encampment. We were having a hilariously good time (on the sly, of course) making them back off by staring at their feet – that always rattles them for some reason – until some bright guy suggested that, after all, that wasn't a very sporting thing to do; we should just let them stare at us undisturbed.
---- THE TRUCK IS COMING---WHOOPEE!

June 2, Chengdu

The Old Truck was delayed yesterday because it was stuck in a hole in the road for a long time. And after we got into it we had to dispatch two of the boys after another one because it ran out of gas. Jimmie tried sitting on the hood and feeding the last drops of the stuff in with a mouth siphon, but it didn't work for long.

So we settled down there where we stopped. It was late in the afternoon, and after playing tag on the paths between the rice paddies for awhile we tried to make ourselves comfortable all over the truck. I was lying on top of the cab, a good position for seeing everybody else as well as the road ahead.

We were just positive we heard the rescue truck coming every five minutes, but it always turned out to be a squeaky water wheel in the stream near by.

It was about nine that we first saw the headlights of our rescue truck striking the trees far ahead. Boy, oh boy, were we happy! And that's about all there was to the trip except that it was pouring rain and midnight when we got here. The Old Truck came in this morning; it would have come last night, following us, but the only headlight it had was a candle that Art held while sitting on the fender!

June 19, Chengdu

I'm going to the States! I'M REALLY GOING TO THE STATES!!!

And I'm really on the way. Dick is staying in Chengdu and then he'll go to India, poor guy.

June 24, Chengdu
I have just said goodbye to Dick and all the Renshow crowd. Goodness, I feel as though I'd lost my eye. They are the nicest people and the best Christians I've ever met.

July, 7
I'm in Calcutta! ----- and I had <u>bananas</u> and toast and <u>butter</u> for breakfast!! And I had so much fun brushing my teeth with that good-tasting toothpaste that I've brushed them twice in the last hour! WHEEEEEEEEEEEEEEEE!
I'm staying at the Lee Memorial House, a Methodist mission girls' school. It's a big airy place with wide verandahs on both sides of the rooms. Indian servants move around quietly and gracefully like nurses in a sick room. Their clothes are flowy and their bright colors and pure whites make things far more colorful than China.

July 8, Calcutta
On July 6th just at dawn, I said goodbye to dear old China and boarded a plane for Calcutta. It wasn't a regular passenger plane, but had aluminum bucket seats for carrying paratroopers. [The seats were lined up with their backs to the windows, facing each other across the aisle, which was stacked with baggage.]
We had a stop-over in Kunming and when we roared off again there were only seven passengers, as most of the crowd had gotten off. It isn't important or anything, but the pilot and I were the only Americans on board.
Soon everybody stretched out and went to sleep – so quickly that when the pilot came through, I was the only one who was able to talk to him. He tripped over my big coolie hat and asked me if was an umbrella or a hat, and that is how the conversation started. We chattered around quite a bit and then ate a can of <u>real Heinz</u> baked beans! Before long I found myself in the co-pilot's seat munching fudge, looking at maps, gaping at the scenery (the Burma Road at this stage) listening on the co-pilot's earphones to a radio program from Berlin, and finding out all about the pilot, who is Captain Royal Leonard.

Then finally –actually—honestly – he had me holding the wheel and managing the plane – altitude 17,000 feet, wings, directions and everything! It was WONDERFUL! I did it only about five minutes by myself, though. I felt so embarrassed and out-of-place that I couldn't keep the old wings straight at all and I had to call the pilot back. (He was somewhere behind me talking to the radio operator-co-pilot guy.)

And then, on top of all this I was absolutely confounded by an invitation out to dinner with the pilot. I didn't know what to make of it, so have since decided to try to seem at least as young as I am (or younger) so as not to excite any more flooring invitations like that.

P.S. I went.

[Note: Over twenty years ago Jonni [my daughter] wrote the whole book: *PS. I Went.* I wish I could put it all here but I'll take some highlights from my diary and wait for the day her book is published.]

Diary: July 9, Calcutta

But flooring as it was, there was the invitation and doubtful and hesitant as I was, there I was, and at 7 o'clock the next evening – [all dolled up for the last time in my white dotted swiss formal.] After tripping on the stairs and breaking the heel off my new white sandals and having to go back for my old Renshow shoes, I found my way in a taxi to the pilot's house. I guess I forgot to mention – Captain Royal Leonard is the youngest senior pilot in the world, possessor of a record 11,000 flying hours to date, Generalissimo Chiang Kai-Shek's private pilot, and the author of the book *I Flew for China*.

The dinner at his house was very formal — everything white, even the chair covers. It was a huge open room with high ceilings and high ceiling fans. A long wide table for about 8 people, and behind each of us was our own servant, who stood at attention through the meal till he swooped forward and removed the plates, or brought a new course so silently I hardly noticed.

After dinner we went to the Grand Hotel where there was an enormous ball room swarming with fancy-dressed people. Capt. Leonard sat me down with a lady who looked like Edna Mae Oliver -– old, elegant and grand, the Patroness of the whole affair, which was a benefit for something or other. She called me "darling" and "dearie" and fussed over me.

When she complained about not being able to see – she couldn't find her glasses – I grandly offered her mine, which was pretty dumb, because I sort of meant it as a joke, but she took me up on it and wore them till I had to ask for them back when we left.

I got really nervous when I saw it was getting on toward 1:00 AM so I told Capt. Leonard I had to go. He was very kind to take me, because I could tell he was really popular there. We rode home in a tonga behind a clopping horse, about an hour back to Lee Memorial.

I was lucky because I sneaked in without waking anybody but the door man -- I didn't have to answer anybody's questions about why I was out so late.

Cinderella could not have had it any better!

Two Canadian families, the Edmonds and the Mitchells at Lee Memorial House were also waiting for passage to the States and/or Canada. When the whole Mitchell family except Mrs. Mitchell came down with colds, she didn't want to miss this rare opportunity to see the Taj Mahal -- she might never be in India again. So her husband agreed that she could go and asked me to go too.

So began another adventure to remember.

July 19, Agra, India

Here I am in Agra, the romantic old city that holds the world-renowned Taj Mahal. I am here with Dr. Helen Mitchell. We got to the Baptist Mission compound here just at dusk; one of those funny little horse-drawn tongas brought us here from the railroad station. All the missionaries from here are off on itineraries somewhere, but some lovely Indian women showed us to this room and cooked an Indian meal for us.

20

It is very hot here and although there are large ceiling fans going, they have moved our beds – mosquito nets and all – out onto the gravel driveway for the night. Already I can hear mosquitoes, as well as wild animals out in the grove of trees behind us.

I had an experience worth remembering last night! Dr. Helen and I had retired for the night on the two upper berths of our compartment on the train, but our two Indian roommates were still awake, with the lights on, below us. I was sound asleep when we stopped in a station, but I woke up with a start when I heard a masculine English voice calling, "Becky!" – or so I thought.

That must be one of the Royal Air Force guys from Chengdu, I thought. I jumped down – thank goodness I was in my housecoat – and was at the open window in a minute.

What did I come face to face with but a whole troop train of British soldiers right on the next track. Horrors! They roared a greeting and I swallowed. "Didn't somebody call me?" I ventured weakly.

Another roar went up. "Call you? Sure and we did that!" They slapped one another on the back and laughed. My face burning, I introduced myself. "A Yank! A Yank! A female Yank!" They slapped each other some more and leaned out their windows.

Well, really I had a good little chat with them, but I was sure glad when our train pulled on – And furthermore, Dr. Helen was about to burst with astonishment at me, a <u>missionary's</u> daughter.

July 20, Agra

I may not be favorably impressed by some things in India, but there is certainly nothing I have ever seen as thrillingly beautiful as the famous old tomb, the Taj Mahal. Honestly, it is dazzling white and so perfect in its formation and surroundings.

It is actually hurt to look at it. We walked toward it as we would walk up to an altar in a great cathedral, reverently silent, just staring.

The pure white marble and many colored inlaid semi-precious stones make it look like something fairies created. But unlike a fairy building it looked as though nothing that ever touched it could prevent if from lasting forever. Somehow simplicity and grandeur and delicate detail are combined to make it something that will never die.

When I could stare no more, I felt as thought I should sit down and rest with my eyes closed; the feeling that they weren't big enough to see it all, the exertion of trying to stretch them, just wore me out.

We climbed up into one of the spires and were breathless at the top of the spiral steps. Wow!

Inside the enormous domed interior, every step and every whisper, even, began to echo back and forth till we were surrounded by a roar of our own making. Incredible!

Around the back of the Taj was a wide white pavement along the river bank; people used to come to the Taj on the river. Out there were a lot of American servicemen sitting around. We had a neat time talking and some of them gave me their addresses to write to their families. One guy gave me a little carved box to send to his mother, and I promised to do it. It sure was fun seeing Americans so far away. They are on leave to get rested up, but they sure are homesick. I hope I get in touch with their families okay.

[End of diary quotes for now.]

As it turned out it was months before I was able to contact them, but my address book came thru what lay ahead and I eventually mailed the little box to the soldier's mother. One family told me that their son had died in battle, but by then I didn't remember which one he was. I was just glad I was able to tell their families about seeing them in India.

In the middle of the South Pacific war, after the fall of Singapore, and with the Indian Ocean alive with Japanese submarines, how were a few civilians to get to the States? We just took our chances, making inquiries wherever we heard we might find a ship. Because I was traveling alone, I hooked up with Mrs. Edmonds and her kids: Art, 19, Robert, 16, and Nettie, 8.

Mrs. Edmonds, a widow, had taught us Latin and world history in Renshow. She was about my height, but plump and round in every direction, and bossy with her brood like a hen with her feathers all puffed out.

Art and I were good friends. He had had polio and was somewhat uncoordinated, but always had a big grin and told lame jokes which usually he was the only one that laughed at when everybody else looked blank.

Robert was a know-it-all and very annoying; Nettie was slow, quite little, and needed a lot of help.

The Mitchells had three little kids; I had hardly known them until Mrs. Mitchell and I made the trip to Agra. She always seemed unhappy, and was hard to talk to. They called her Dr. Mitchell, but she wasn't really a full-fledged doctor.

The ten of us, Edmonds, Mitchells, and I were a "package deal" to travel together.

The last day before leaving Calcutta I bought a Bible. I had met Robert and Eugene Morse, missionary brothers about my age from Northern Burma. These fellows inspired me tremendously because they had seen REAL action, I thought. They had encouraged me to get a Bible and helped me pick it out. I had never seen a concordance before and was quite excited to look up things to read.

The Ship Trips

Diary: August 3, 1943: Shipboard, Bay of Bengal
This is a British freighter, the *HMS Querimba* and we are headed for Sydney, Australia. The cargo is mostly hemp. All the portholes and outside doors are completely blacked out at night with two layers of heavy black curtains. You have to go through one and be sure it's closed before you go through the next one. The Captain is tall and thin with white hair and quite intimidating. He's had two ships sunk under him so far in the war and that makes him nervous about everything.

The ship has only four passenger cabins and we fill them all. They open right into the saloon where we have meals and do everything else. I'm rooming with Mrs. Edmonds and Nettie.
There isn't much to do. Mrs. Edmonds thinks she ought to teach us physics so we'll be caught up with something or other when we all get back into school. The Chief Engineer looked doubtful when she suggested to him that we all go into the engine room to see how things work. I wish she'd just forget she is a teacher sometimes.
We are always zigzagging to outsmart the Japanese, which means that you can't be sure which side of the ship is east or west or north or south and the crew is mostly Muslims, so several times a day they put their prayer rugs out on the deck and bow down to Mecca. The guys at the wheel usually pick this time to run the ship in circles, almost, just to confuse them about where Mecca is. I feel kinda sorry for them, shifting their rugs around while they are praying.

August 12, Shipboard
I wonder what Mom and Dad really feel about my going to the States. I guess they are in favor of it. However I wish I could have talked it all over with them before leaving. Telegrams and letters were so inadequate that sometimes I was at a terrible loss trying to think out what <u>right</u> thing to do.
I wonder what it will be like when I get to Chicago! When I'm <u>really</u> <u>there</u> and see Aunt T and Uncle Percy. Should I just show up and say "Hello" or will it be better to be met? What will they look like? I think I'll call them long distance the first chance I get.... it makes me all fuzzy-wuzzy inside. But, boy, I'll tell the world that it sure is swell of them to take me in (at least, I hope they do.) I'm going to try to be good (`-`).

August, Friday the 13th, Shipboard
　　I don't believe in that Friday-the-thirteenth superstition, anyway, and besides it's too nice a day to worry about <u>what</u> day it is. Days are days wherever they are – and a nice day's a day you don't worry in -- whatever it is.
　　I copied out the words of a hymn on a piece of paper and stuffed it up under the steel beam over my bunk. It was *When you Trust and Obey*. I wonder who will find it, and I hope it will comfort him if he's scared or homesick.

August 25, Shipboard
　　I was feeling so energetic that I went out on the hatch and tried to teach Margy and Peter how to stand on their heads. Neither they nor I succeeded very well. Pretty soon Mr. Mitchell tried to do it, and then, before we knew what was happening, there was our highly respected Captain standing a perfect headstand in front of us! Wow! Were we ever surprised!

September 5, still on the bounding main
　　We had a church service this morning; Mr. Mitchell led again. His sermon particularly impressed me because he said that we Christians have prayed, "Thy kingdom come, Thy will be done on earth as it is in heaven," and have sat back and left it at that. We have to <u>do</u> the will of God, he said, and I believe we do too. For how else is anything lasting good ever going to come about if we don't get busy and work for it?
　　And that's how I've been so inadequate a Christian lately. I've been reading the fifth and sixth chapters of Matthew the last few days. My, but they are marvelous. They show up my own mistakes in so many places that I just want to read them over and over again to let them soak in.
　　I've been angry at people without cause, I've spoken sharply, I've been selfish and done a million other things that Christ said not to do, but now that I've read that, I'm going to start all over again and I hope everybody else who reads it feels the same way. It certainly is the most comforting and helpful and teaching thing there ever was to have something to go to when one's been bad like me!

　　[More diary quotes will follow soon...]

Loaded offshore in Sydney we bade farewell to the friends we had made on the almost seven week trip from Calcutta, and found a small hotel where again we followed every lead to obtain passage to the States. In the meantime Mrs. Edmonds didn't fail to drag us to every museum or educational spot available, much to my disgust. I was happier going to the movies, and discovered *Gone with the Wind* which I watched at least twice.

One or two of the ship's officers took me to movies or ice skating, and on the night before the *Querimba* left port again, Mac, the Third Engineer presented me with a delicate wrist watch with a mother-of-pearl face as we stood in the doorway of the hotel. I was thrilled with the gift but told him he shouldn't do that. He insisted I keep it because he wanted me to have it -- and asked me for a kiss. Grateful as I was I declined to give it to him and warmly shook his hand instead.

One of the CIM ladies, Elizabeth Swanton, who had crossed China with us, was from Sydney, so I looked up her family through the CIM office there. As a result I spent a delightful Sunday at their Baptist church with her aunt and uncle, and Ruth, who was Elizabeth's sister. It was a warm wonderful time, so encouraging for me to have made new friends, even for a day.

We found passage on a freighter sailing from Brisbane, so departed Sydney on the train. I had fallen in love with the beautiful city, but could hardly wait to be finally going "home" even though HOME still meant China.

Diary: September 25, Shipboard
It's going to be swell to be on the ocean again! It's a beautiful Swedish ship, the *SS Mirabooka*, named for a constellation in the Southern Hemisphere. Belonging to a neutral nation, it is not camouflaged with horrible grey paint. It shines and glistens, so dazzlingly white that it just makes me feel good inside. There is a huge vertical yellow and blue Swedish flag painted from the deck rail all the way to the water line. They for sure don't want to be mistaken for a war ship.

We are blacked out at night, but the regulations are not nearly as stringent as they were on the last ship. In fact it seems silly because although the portholes and doors are blacked up, people are allowed to smoke on deck and the engine hatches are open.

There are twenty six passengers, the Mitchells and Edmonds included. Some of them, about seven girls, are war brides married to American soldiers they met in Australia, headed to join them in the States. I asked one of the girls what her husband was like and she said she couldn't quite remember because they knew each other such a short time!

September 26
　　　　The Society Crowd is crooning very mooningly upstairs in the smoking room and lounge. The girls wear tons of red lipstick and sing really awful bawdy songs, like they are in a bar all the time. They start at the breakfast table, flirting with the officers, and keep it up really loud all through the day. If things are going on all over the world like things that have been going on here there will <u>never</u> be a decent world. It is <u>so</u> hard to be a <u>real</u> Christian in it all. I re-dedicated myself hard and fast tonight and I <u>know</u> that God's guiding me this time.
　　　　The Holdridges, mother, and son Henry, are the only other Americans aboard. Henry had a job with the Australian government, and although he has been there only two years, he has picked up the Aussie "aiksent." Mrs. Holdridge is a regular old New Yorker, just hates Australia and wishes Henry had never brought her there, had never picked up "Australian-ism" and never engaged himself to an Aussie girl.

September 26, Bed time
　　　　Tonight Henry and I let ourselves out through the blackout curtains and went out to see the stars. They are incredible – I can hardly believe how many there are! Then as we were leaning against the rail, he told me – and <u>swore</u> me to secrecy – that he is secretly married to an Australian girl, but he won't tell his mother till he gets her back to White Plains. He says she would have a fit if she knew. It sounded very romantic and sad. Then I asked him her name. Can you believe it – he is <u>married to Elizabeth Swanton's sister Ruth!</u> And I met her just a few days ago in Sydney! Is that ever a coincidence!! Ruth will follow sometime later – I hope it won't be too long. Wow!

September 27
　　　　Oh, fooey. Tonight I don't feel like much. Doggone it, something's come over me lately. I thought that two nights ago I'd gotten over it all, but I'm still just as bad as I ever was. I resolve to be a Christian one day and tell myself that this time I mean it, but I no sooner do than I'm just as sloppy as ever about

it right all over again. I guess I'm just a weak sinful person. Christ said the spirit was willing but the flesh was weak. Oh, I wish I could be like Him! He had to struggle too, but he had the strength to come out on top. If I come out on top this time I'll certainly be grateful a long time afterwards.

[A word from God...?]
Becky, I'm with you all the time. I'm here, right here, all the time. Don't worry, Becky, you're willing and you see your failures and your mistakes. I won't let you stay far from the right. There's a lot of sin in the world; you're seeing some of the deepest of it these days on shipboard. You're willing to work against it. But don't worry now. I'll prepare you so that someday you'll be able to do a part in the bettering of your world and your children's children's world. Lo, I am with you always, even unto the end of your days.

I know Christ will help. All I need is more strength, more experience, and more faith. How wonderful the Christian religion is! What hope do men have without it?

September 30, South Pacific
The jacket of the book I just threw overboard said that soldiers needed books. "Send them this book when you've finished reading it." Bah! I wouldn't send anyone that book any more than I would send him a piece of second hand chewing gum! This is war time -- a time when people need something firm to build them up. What is a soldier going to become like when he lives in sin, without having to mess up his mind with trash in a book.

It makes me so mad – but most of all it makes me resolve, more than anything else, to start someday soon to write a book, and not a trashy one – it could be about our travels and the "All of a sudden Terrys"-- only all true.

Later: Some of the passengers are just fine and others have an awful patronizing way about them. ... Isn't it funny the way you can get along so well with some and others you can get along so well without!

The captain of this ship is a fat guy who likes the girls. He was strutting around in shorts before we left port, inviting them to have a drink with him. Now some of the girls have moved their mattresses up on the boat deck! I don't even want to know what is going on up there.

October 6, Shipboard, of course

Henry pretended at breakfast that someone put salt into his bed last night. He rubbed his back up and down the chair, complaining that it had gotten into his sunburn and is killing him. When he left the table he stopped and blamed Mac and Siscow are sore at Art and Robert because they think they're responsible for the salt. Whoa! Wouldn't they boil if they knew there had never been any salt at all.

I spent my spare time writing **Another one! Shame on you!** in the bottom of the ash tray. Tonight somebody had put it in front of Daphne's place at supper.

After supper while the drinking party was going on, Robert and I sneaked into the pantry to see what went on there. The Society Gang is celebrating crossing the Equator in the saloon. Oke, the waiter, was just getting more drinks ready to take upstairs.

I picked up a bottle of beer and tipped it over the sink. "What would happen if I dumped this out? Would I have to pay for it?"

"I'm afraid you would," he grinned.

"Then it isn't worth it." So I put the bottle back on the tray.

We helped ourselves to some olives and cherries then took down two small wine glasses and drank some water to the Captain's health: that he might behave himself, then toodle-do, 10:15 off to bed.

October 7

Last night we may have had a doodly evening, but it didn't end up quite so doodly. I wonder how I'm still here!

We all went to bed and slept as lack-a-dazical and free and easy as we ever are. At one o'clock we were awakened by a violent banging on the door and Mr. Stack's voice yelling, "EVERYBODY OUT! EVERYBODY OUT! THE SHIP'S BURNING!"

I rolled over in bed, thinking it was a practical joke of some kind, until Mrs. Edmonds screamed, "WAKE UP, NETTIE, THE SHIP'S ON FIRE!"

I sat up and put on my glasses and watch, reached for my housecoat and put it on. By the time I was down from my bunk Mrs. Edmonds had cleaned out entirely. Her voice crying "LIFE BELTS, LIFE BELTS!" grated on my mind, though, and I ran my hand back and forth on the top shelf of the wardrobe, frantically trying to reach my belt in the dark. I found it on the floor finally, and dismissing the thought of grabbing my get-a-way bag, I rushed out into the corridor.

And it was no joke. Pouring from the pantry and stairs direction heavy grey smoke rolled down toward me, lighted up horribly like a sunset by red bursts of flames. I rushed down toward the deck in the other direction, only to be met by more heavy smoke, this time mixed with sharp voices.

"Which way? Which way?" I yelled, feeling utterly alone.

"Up the companion way, girlie," somebody said.

There were a couple of people up there yelling and crying. "It's all right, it's all right, Nettie," I said, trying to stop her crying.

"How did it start" I yelled at everybody.

The smoke got thicker and thicker on the boat deck. Mrs. Edmonds was out of control entirely. "Robert, ARTHUR, ROBERT, ARTHUR! Where are you?" she kept screaming "Becky, where are you?"

"Here I am," I said, "I'm all right." She nearly crushed my hand in hers. I let go and pressed against the rail between the lifeboats trying to get air. Once I fell on my knees with a violent choking of smoke and stayed there a second to pray. Somehow I wasn't afraid the whole time. Somehow I knew that God would take care of us, and He did.

Suddenly a burst of flames lit up the deck fore of the funnel. People began to scream again: LOWER THE LIFEBOATS! HELP! HELP!

Henry was just grand all the way through it. "Take it easy, people: now you're all going to be all right; nobody will be hurt," he kept saying, calmly, loudly, firmly, and clearly.

But the flames got brighter and smoke much denser and still no member of the crew appeared to answer the demand for a LIFEBOAT! LIFEBOAT!

[Except the captain appeared on the bridge deck and yelled down to us to come up there – it would be safe up there! But no one paid any attention — he was obviously drunk. Fire was coming out right under him and around the life belt chests. I helped Henry find a life jacket, but it was a child size and pushed his arms up in a crazy way. – We had never had a life boat drill on this ship.]

Stack and Misco took over and began to work the [lifeboat] crank. But the boat they worked on (#3) stuck at a crucial moment [The pulleys were solid paint!]. Art and I meanwhile were working fiercely on the crank of the other boat (#1) praying all the time.

The number three boat finally got loose, so we ran over there, and before long everyone was scrambling madly into it as it lowered down level with the deck.

The boat swung loose and we waited for the drop, but there was panic when only the stern fell. We were dangling from the bow by a single rope many feet above the water. At first we were just a tangled mass of people hanging on desperately and screaming senselessly for their lives.

October 8

Gradually people slid down and fell off into the water. Mrs. Edmonds called, "Nettie! Nettie! NETTIE!" as she fell in. Mrs. Holdridge was beyond herself in pain. My weight was crushing her against a seat. "Oh, Henry, oh, Henry, oh, Henry!" she kept moaning. [She had broken her arm.] Mr. Mitchells' foot was crushed between a seat and the fifty gallon water tank, which had slid forward, nearly killing him with pain, but keeping him out of the water. I held on to two ropes for dear life and was one of the few who didn't fall out.

Finally, when we thought we could hold on no longer and were hoarse from yelling, "Hold on!" someone above us hit the rope with a hatchet. The boat fell with such a crash that I thought certainly everyone was killed. My head banged against a seat, knocking me out for a second or two.

I sat up and looked around: the boat was already full of water. People all around were screaming desperately. I saw Mr. Mitchell lying face down, his hair kind of floating around his head. I thought certainly he was dead. I screamed his name, tumbled over things, turned his head out of the water and slapped his cheek. "Are you all right?"

He sort of shook himself awake and said, "Yeah, I guess so, but I can't move till you get his damn water tank off my foot." I moved toward his foot and started working, but couldn't budge it an inch.

I don't know exactly what happened next, but then I saw Mrs. Edmonds struggling desperately in the water. She seemed to be completely hysterical, calling and screaming and struggling in the water. I reached out to her, but another rough wave carried her away from the boat. "Mrs. Edmonds! MRS. EDMONDS!" I screamed.

Then Art was in the water struggling beside her to push her closer to the boat. She looked like death itself [and her get-away-bag which she always wore around her neck was bobbing up and down under her chin.] I screamed her name again as an ironic thought passed through my mind: that's how it's done in the movies.

I was thinking of jumping in for her, but I knew it would only complicate matters. Somehow, though, my hand reached her and I tugged her into the boat. I think somebody helped me, but I'm not sure. I couldn't possibly have pulled in her weight unaided.

Gradually the boat filled up again. People everywhere were calling and crying. "Where's Belle; where's Nettie? Are you all right, Margy? Robert? Robert? Where are you, Robert?" Everybody began to call for Robert. I didn't expect to hear him answer, but from the deck above he called down. I looked up and saw him silhouetted against the red glow that the cabins were.

"I'm all right. I'm okay!" he called.

We were sitting in water up to our waists. "Start bailing," somebody yelled. And we started. Hands, hats, everything we could hold we used. But the water washed in as fast as we chucked it out. [What we didn't realize then was that the boat had cracked apart from bow to stern and was held together by the thwarts and kept afloat by air tanks.]

[There were some comical sidelines too. When Henry grabbed the side of the boat, he looked at me and said, "Oh, Becky, I've just lost my thirty-two shilling hat!" Then when he got seated he announced, wiggling his pajama top down over his hips. "I hope you ladies aren't shy because I lost my pajama bottoms too," There he sat and proceeded to throw up.]

People were crying, people were yelling, people were choking with seasickness, people half mad seemed to be everywhere. The boat banged up against the ship each rise and fall of the waves, lifting and dropping us fifteen feet each time.

[It was during this plunging up and down that Art performed the most heroic act of all. Realizing that Nettie was in the water between the ship and the lifeboat when it hit the water, he grabbed her, ducked under the water, holding her till the boat had passed over their heads, banged the side of the ship, and had fallen away again. Then he boosted her into it and dove down himself to avoid being hit by the next crash against the side. Without a doubt he saved Nettie's life that night.]

Later when we had drifted up to the forecastle, still attached to the ship by a rope, somebody threw down some raincoats and comforting words that the fire would soon be under control. However, the bridge was fully and fiercely ablaze; pieces of it were crumbling and falling, but the wind blew all the smoke and pieces toward the port side. Way down in the lifeboat we could feel the intense heat.

Somebody above realized our hopeless condition and told us to get out of the way of the raft. Mr. Misco and I and a couple of others pushed the boat along with oars against the side of the ship and moved us up a little ways. Then the raft shot into the water with a boom, barely missing us. It was attached to our lifeboat somehow, so we pulled it in. All the wounded people and kids were moved over to it. Art, Misco, Mr. Mitchell and I were the only ones left in the lifeboat.

Mr. Mitchell's foot was still crushed by the water tank. Somebody handed the painter of the raft over to me. I held it tight, but sometimes I thought it would tear the skin off my hands.

Then Art started humming. I'd been humming off and on too, but to hear him made it even better. We began singing — everything we could think of that wouldn't make the situation worse.

Time was no element. By the glow of the fire I could see that my watch had stopped at ten minutes after one. We may have been there several hours, or only one, I don't know. Toward early dawn, though, the fire was under control and they sent down a rope ladder for us to come back up. Being in the lifeboat, I was the nearest and the first to go up. A strong Swede, came down, and tied a rope around my waist. I stood on the edge of the lifeboat and tried to time a jump for the ladder with the rise and fall of the boat. After several attempts I grabbed the bottom of the ladder, and another sailor pulled me up step by step to the deck.

And did the ship feel good! – even though the deck was pretty warm and made me want to hurry across. I wound my way to the stern [poop deck] where somebody led me to where the other passengers were collected. [None of the brides had even headed for the boat deck in the first place, never having been on a ship or having had a life boat drill. They instead had headed for the poop, where their friendly crew was. Probably some lives were saved that way.]

One of the crew told me to go down to his cabin and help myself to some of his clothes - - Oh, they felt *so* warm! Man's pants that I rolled up at the bottom and a big sweat shirt. I'd been in my nightgown and my housecoat, which is completely shrunk now, the dumb thing, and I'll never wear it again.

Mr. Stack was the first to notice the fire. It started in the officers' quarters on the port side and blew up a regular wind tunnel to the upper decks. If he had not given the signal when he did all of us would have burned. One more minute in there would have lost us!

We have been surveying the damage; the mid-ship – saloon, kitchen, everything on top is burned completely; the bridge and all the navigation equipment gone; on the port decks all the passenger cabins and officers quarters are gone—a ghost of a mess. But on the starboard side, after burning through the wardrobe and all our clothes, the fire stopped half way through our cabin. The books in the drawers on the other side are smoky but okay. There has been an awful lot of water up there but it is gradually draining out. My get-a-way bag was on the floor – my passport, Renshow diary, and other stuff, is completely soaked.

Yesterday afternoon Mr. Mitchell, hobbling on a make shift crutch, held a short service and buried the Chief Engineer who suffocated and was burned to death in his cabin, where the fire started. They wrapped his body in a flag and slid it overboard. It took some time for it to sink -- we watched it bob up and down for a while and it was very sad. He hadn't seen his wife in nearly four years, and he had a three year old son he'd never seen.

Putting it Together

After everyone on the ship had realized what had happened and the wounded were treated as best we could --- well, I should stop here and explain that there was no doctor on board except "Dr. Helen" Mitchell who had given up medical school to marry Mr. Mitchell. At times she was quite bitter about that, but in the emergency on shipboard she pitched in like a pro.

She set Mrs. Holdridge's arm and comforted her as best she could because her injury was the worst of anyone: for when the sailors were trying to get her up from the water the rope ladder had swung her against the side of the ship and bashed her head! Poor lady, she was so traumatized.

A couple of big strong crew members had descended the rope ladder to rescue Mr. Mitchell who was still sitting in the water, pinned by the water drum. The guys were able to release his leg and carry him up to the deck. All of us did the best we could to comfort them both till we got to the hospital in Honolulu -- and Dr. Helen gave them lots of brandy.

The rest of us, some crew and all the passengers, camped on the rear deck under a tarp slung across a boom. This wasn't a simple matter because the deck was stacked with 50-gallon drums of linseed oil which had to be covered first with boards. Even though we were still at the equator and the nights weren't cold, everyone seemed to shiver and shake from shock.

I was sleeping in a roll of blankets and next to me was a Swede about my age, who didn't speak English. Part way through the night he rolled over and without a word put his arm around me, blanket and all. It was so comforting to be hugged that I slept peacefully the rest of the night.

Next morning, Mrs. Edmonds, knowing nothing about my innocent comfort, blew her stack because nobody had thought to separate the men from the women! Believe me, she saw to it that by the next night things were prim and proper. She had a few other fits, though, which made me wish Mom was there instead of her!

One of the crew members, Jenson, went to his cabin, which was in tact, and brought me a white dress box. "Here, I want you to have this," he said. Inside was a beautiful jersey dress with a bright red flower print, and a pair of stockings. Obviously it was a gift he was taking home to his girlfriend.

With the cabins gone, everything happened publicly on the deck. Well! When Mrs. Edmonds saw him giving me the box, she marched up to me and said, "Becky Jean Terry, WHAT would your mother say?"

"Well," I answered bravely, "I think under the circumstances she would be very happy for me to have a dress." But I doubt she heard me.

Lucky for me I hadn't shown her what was in the box. So I pulled my benefactor aside and told him I was going to fix her. I took the box to my bed and hid the dress under the covers. Then when I knew she was watching I went to the ship's rail where Jenson was standing, pretended to apologize to him, and gave him back the box. He shook his head and looked at her sadly. Then he dropped the empty box overboard.

Later Jenson and I had a good laugh, and Mrs. Edmonds was satisfied that I hadn't committed the unforgivable sin.

When she was out of the picture later on, I wore the dress all through the next few years — it was a special souvenir of a very good memory.

One day I helped Oke peel potatoes. The food supplies in the refrigerator lower decks were okay, and food began to appear. I don't remember where they cooked it, probably on the poop, or whether we had a table or ate off plates on our laps, but food wasn't a problem -- whoever was in charge saw to that.

The Captain, though, was up to his old tricks, where there was an auxiliary wheel and some navigation equipment at the poop. After the ship had wallowed a couple of days till the engine room was bailed out and working, the captain held court, as it were, on the poop deck. He usually had at least one girl at his side, but two was more common. I'll not forget the night five days later when we approached the Big Island of Hawaii: There we were, a crippled derelict ship with no radio communication showing up unannounced a few miles from Pearl Harbor. We could have been blasted out of the water at any minute!

A signal light was flashing in the distance, and there was the captain signaling back, his left arm around one bride and his right around another bride and a flashlight in his middle!

Later that night we suddenly realized there were two destroyers escorting us, only a few hundred yards away, one on each side. They were so totally silent that we didn't even know at first they had showed up. But Henry, realizing who they were, cupped his hands around his mouth and shouted out at the top of his lungs, "Hey, you guys! Who won the World Series?"

There was a flutter of laughter from the destroyer on our port side; then somebody shouted, "SHUT UP!!" Dead silence again. I turned to Henry and said, "What is the World Series?" I'd never heard of it.

The Red Cross greeted us in Honolulu, took us to their warehouse and gave us all new clothes, coats, dresses, underwear, everything we needed, then drove us to a shoe store and bought us shoes.

The passengers were put up in the Moana Hotel, but after a couple of days I went to stay with my cousins, which was a huge surprise for them and a big blessing for me.

On one of my visits back to the hotel, the Manager called me into his office. "How well do you know Australians?" He asked me.

"Only a little, just the girls off the ship, I guess..."

"Well!" he said. "These ladies are causing so much trouble we have decided not to let any Australians stay here again!"

All I could do was nod. Yes, I could imagine that they had been having a gay old time with the hotel guests, just as they had with the crew and officers on the ship. I had noticed that when we went to the Red Cross warehouse they had picked out the fanciest dresses, and at the shoe store, the highest heels possible. ... oh, well....!

Because I wasn't staying in the hotel -- and thereby, I thought, saving them money -- I persuaded the ship's company to fly me the rest of the way. Actually, the US powers that be had forbidden any Americans to travel on that ship again, though the girls were all waiting to re-embark.

So the last leg of my journey was flying on the Clipper Ship --22 hours at very low altitude – to Treasure Island.

Surprise! What do you think the headlines in the San Francisco Call Bulletin were proclaiming on the newsstands?

EXTRA!!
Dramatic Fire at Sea Told Here

Sure enough, there were pictures of five of the brides looking very prim and happy and front page descriptions of what I knew all too well. I could have adjusted some details, which I properly corrected – in my scrapbook: all the things I thought they'd gotten wrong. But after all, everybody on the ship saw it through different eyes, and all had different stories to tell. I'm just thankful I'm still alive to tell you mine.

The first chance I had, I found a phone book and looked up Aunt T's cousin Marie Tight, who I'd met in San Francisco on our way back to China in 1940. She was flabbergasted that I'd showed up from nowhere, but of course collected me, took me home, and pampered me very nicely.

There was another hurdle to jump in that simply getting a train to Chicago wasn't simple, as troops had priority and so forth. But fortunately Mr. Tight has a lot of pull and wrangled a ticket for me to Chicago -- via Dallas, Forth Worth.

And by way of closure, before I left San Francisco I was interviewed by a maritime review board regarding the Mirabooka disaster, in particular the captain. The board – don't remember the official name -- later revoked the captain's license and effectually prevented him from ever going to sea again.

So after connecting with more dumbfounded cousins – Mom's in Fort Worth -- and a few more minor adventures, I made it by train to the waiting arms of Aunt T and Uncle Percy in Chicago.

Aaahh! (a big sigh!) Home at last -- Just in time for Thanksgiving dinner!

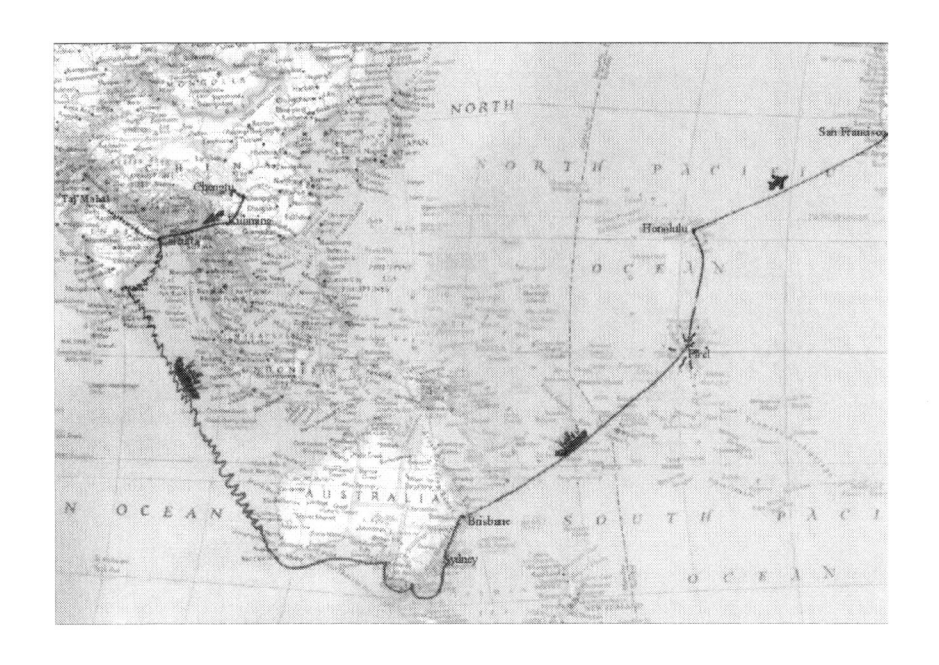

I made it! 20,000 miles in 170 days = 117.65 miles a day = approximately 4.9 miles an hour. Quite a trip!

Culture Shock

1943: Being in America and looking like everybody else, yet feeling out of place, homesick, and being quite out of touch with my peers, took a lot of adjustment. Probably, it was as big an adjustment for Aunt Teressa and Uncle Percy, as for me!

They had a modern cement block house on a pretty, wide street in Riverside, Illinois, west of Chicago. They had never had anybody but each other, and though well set in their ways, they were good and kind to me. Aunt T bought me a winter coat, skirts, and sweaters, and shook her head in disgust at the too big olive green wool dress, with moth holes in the skirt, that her cousin Marie Tight had given me in San Francisco. "Humph! She could afford to dress you in mink," she puffed.

She helped me sort through my smoky stuff from the fire and insisted I throw away the stuffed mongoose which I'd bought from a street kid in Madras. The tin trunk I'd bought in Calcutta had survived the fire because it was in a small forward hold of the ship. Thus my few treasures from China and souvenirs from India made it to Chicago.

The weather in Shanghai and in West China had never been as severe as Chicago, so one of the most difficult adjustments for me was to walk to school in the snow. Okay, you hear exaggerated stories of kids trudging through three miles of snow to get to school, well I really did – though only 1.89 miles.

I had my first pair of long pants, wool slacks, that I pulled up under my skirt for the walk, then stored them in my locker till the walk home. Some days my knees were red raw from cold and chapping from the wool, then in the school building which seemed so overheated, I perspired so much my wool sweaters got ruined under the arms. Funny things to remember, I know, but they stand out as some of my discomfort in getting acclimatized to the States.

Furthermore, Aunt Teressa, being a dietitian, took it on herself to strip me of the ten extra pounds I had gained on the long shipboard trips with four and five course meals. When Mom found out that she was giving me such skimpy meals she wrote that I needed to have "something that sticks to her ribs" and admonished her long distance to take better care of me. True, I hated taking to school sandwiches made with only lettuce and mayonnaise and nothing tasty inside.

Arriving at Riverside-Brookfield High School in the middle of the winter with nothing but my word that I was a senior, the school took me at face value and let me in. I guess I really was an oddity because the girls insisted, first off, that I needed to wear lipstick. I resisted and resisted, even though one or two of them bought me "lighter colors" as a gift. Lipstick was something I really couldn't get used to as it always brought forth vivid images of Australian brides I had no respect for.

    My classroom experiences were a mixture of social ineptness on my part and eyebrow-raising by my classmates. In one class we were required to read the Readers' Digest and report on it. In one discussion over the plight of Negroes I stood up for them saying they had every right to do so and so... just as we had. A girl named Jenna, turned to me in horror, and as we left the class she was waiting at the door. Clutching her books to her chest, she snarled through her teeth, "I...hope....all... your...kids...turn...out....to.. be...NIGGERS!" and stomped away in the opposite direction.

    In Miss Courtney's math class just after we were all seated and ready one morning, I raised my hand: "Miss Courtney, I don't have my lesson prepared for today." In an instant it seemed the whole class looked around aghast at me, their mouths dropped open.

    Miss Courtney sized up the situation and said, "Well, Becky Terry I'm proud of you. I don't know if this has ever happened in this class before. How may of the rest of you would like to confess that you haven't done your homework?"

    There were a few self-conscious snickers, as a lot of kids slid down in their seats.

    After the class one of the boys stopped me, 'WHY in heck would you tell a teacher THAT?"

    In another class a frilly blonde named Cynthia was complaining about butter rationing because of the war. I spoke up and stopped the whole class. "You don't have a clue what war is all about! Have you seen refugees that have nothing at all to eat? Have you ever been bombed? Have you ever seen a whole city burned down? Have you ever been on a battle field and seen dead bodies rotting? You just don't know how good you have it in your cozy little Riverside, Illinois!"

    Well, it was a sort of dividing line. Some kids were my friends and some avoided me like poison.

    Frank Sinatra was all the rage, and after one weekend a bunch of kids came to school raving about one of his concerts in downtown Chicago. I asked one of them, "Who is Frank Sinatra?" Well, obviously I was about the dumbest kid they'd ever met. "Don't you know ANYTHING?"

But when they had elections for the student council and I listened to the insipid speeches of the candidates I decided to run, and gave a blazing speech that we needed change in this school and they should elect me – which much to my amazement they did! That caused more hard feelings because they thereby unseated the school superintendent's daughter Barbara B. who had thought the position was her absolute right.

By spring I had friends to walk home with, and I still keep in touch with two of them: Carol Smith who went on to be an opera singer in Milan, Italy, and Isabel Thompson who is a faithful letter writer and rare friend, who read all the Terry Letters a few years ago.

After graduation I wanted to go to college right away. I had received over three hundred dollars from the Transatlantic Shipping Company as settlement for my stuff lost in the fire -- enough for the summer semester at Oberlin College.

So began my broader education, although I might argue it was already pretty broad.

Oberlin, in Ohio, is an historic liberal arts college established in 1833. It was liberal in that it was the first in the US to regularly admit female and black students. I didn't know anything about its history, it just sounded like a nice place to go.

I liked it there, and was assigned to the old girl's dorm: Lord Cottage. My search for learning was not so much for knowledge as for where I belonged. I had a nice room to myself on the third floor which I decorated with my Chinese pictures, carved box, and porcelain horses, my small book collection, and a bedspread I dyed gold in the dorm basement, to match the gold curtains.

My dorm mates were a mixture: a girl from New Jersey who always walked down the hall with her soap and towel, stark naked, when headed for the showers, to Barbara and Beverly, prim and proper identical twins. They deserve more mention because they had --or tried to have-- a big influence on my future.

Barbara had had polio which left one leg much shorter than the other. She always walked leaning on Beverly, who was her guide and her protector. They had come as music majors after being Gospel singers for a time on the "Back to the Bible" radio show. And as Baptists they were very much concerned that I needed to be saved.

However, the more they tried to straighten me out by telling me I needed to be born again, the more I resisted. All I could see was that they didn't believe in lipstick, but carefully applied it, then wiped if off before they started out to take on the world. Just a pink glow, that's all, not real lipstick.

One day while we were in the dining hall, I saw them tipping their heads together whispering about something. I asked them what the secret was. Then they looked up and nodded in the direction of a very handsome fellow at another table. "You see David over there? He's a JEW!"

This was a shock. I had a sweet friend Irene Steinman in Shanghai who was a refugee from Germany, but I had not thought it was a bad thing. That they should be so strongly against a very handsome innocent guy just because he was Jewish was an entirely new prejudice I'd never experienced.

The twins roomed across the hall from me so I dropped in and visited with them quite a lot. A Sadie Hawkins dance was coming up, the one where the girls invite the boys. One night there was quite a discussion going on there with several girls as to which boys they would invite to the dance. A particular boy, Joel, who I had met, seemed to be everybody's choice but no one had decided whether to ask him. So I quietly decided I would invite him myself. I had bought some material and made my own formal for the party; so all I needed was a date.

Joel showed up with a hand picked bouquet of daises; we walked across the campus to the party, had a rather shy time together, walked back to the dorm and shook hands at the door. We told each other thanks for the nice time and said goodnight.

However, I guess some of the girls were upset at my jumping the gun on them, because when I came home, my room was completely trashed. I could barely step through the door. My clothes were thrown out of my dresser drawers, the drawers were on the floor, the curtains were pulled down, my bed torn apart-- the bedding and mattress on the floor, my pencils and papers strewn about --every possible thing messed up, even my pictures pulled off the wall -- everything, just short of dumping out my ink.

I was absolutely devastated. Nothing like that had ever happened. In Renshow; even with all the high-jinks we thought up, we would never have done such a stupid unkind thing to anyone. I was so shocked and hurt I resolved not to acknowledge to <u>anybody</u> that it had happened. I carefully put things back in order, went to bed and never mentioned a word to anyone. I wasn't about to give them the satisfaction of having gotten some kind of revenge on me -- whatever their motives and whoever they were.

As the summer wore on, in spite of what I labeled the twins' hypocrisy, I was bothered by their harping on this born again idea. Nobody had ever told me I needed to be saved or born again. I was a Christian. I was being a Good Girl. Being Christian was being good, being nice and doing good things for God. I couldn't relate to the twins, but they had pointed out that it said in the Bible I needed to be born again.

One night I climbed out on the wrought iron fire escape outside my window and sat in the moonlight with a notebook. I looked at the stars as my mind wondered over the question. I remember the furlough year in Ohio when we took "Sunday drives" to see the fall colors. Often we would drive by old barns that had JESUS SAVES painted on the roofs. I remembered thinking, saved from what?

I thought of a missionary who had once stopped overnight at South Gate. He seemed to have a glow about him that I had never seen on anyone before. I don't remember what he talked about but as he sat at the dinner table I couldn't keep but wondering why he was so ... different. Now, I wondered, was he born again?

My notebook was no use; it wasn't light enough even if I had anything to write. I just sat in the night pondering what born again meant. I didn't have enough respect for the twins to ask them; I didn't know a minister; my parents weren't nearby, but surely if they knew they would have told me. I threw the question out to the sky, but there was no answer.

Then I remembered the time on the ship when I wrote in my diary what it seemed God was telling me: that he was with me all the time. Was it God talking to me or me talking to myself? I thought of the Swede who had hugged me so gently after the fire, the guy I never saw again. I wondered if he could have been an angel God sent since I hadn't had a hug in such a long time.

I gradually reviewed everything that happened when the ship burned. Something I remembered when I was hanging suspended over the water came back in graphic detail. It was the moment when the boat broke loose and started dumping people into the water.

As I was hanging there, my glasses fell off. I had thought, Oh NO! How can I ever get along without my glasses! Yet, a while later I realized they were right back on my face. How could that be? Did God pick them out of the ocean and give them back to me, or was it my imagination that they fell off? No, I was sure they fell off because the panic of losing my glasses was very real.

But something else: I remembered the terrified thought while hanging there: "This is how it feels to die!" And I saw looking up at me hundreds of red faces, surrounded by fire, all kinds of faces jammed together with frightened expressions, and I felt as though I was somehow <u>one</u> with everyone who had ever died and was about to fall into a terrible pit with them! It was a horrible picture. Then when the boat crashed into the water it disappeared. This night, almost a year later, it came back as vividly as the first time I saw it.

God, were you showing me a glimpse of hell? Is it a real place? I know I'm not going there because I've been a good Christian all my life – or have I?

No answer. Just the beautiful starlit night, getting cool around me. I began to shiver, so I crawled back inside and went to bed. Well, I guess I'll figure it out some other time, and eventually went to sleep.

The Folks' Place

The Terry family that had once been so close together was now scattered everywhere. Dad and Mother had gone from south China to India where they were waiting for a way to get to the States. Dan was sailing the Atlantic in the Merchant Marines while his family, Muriel, Mike and Pete, were in New York. Warny was in Ohio at Antioch College. Dick, back from his adventures in India, was with Aunt T and Uncle Percy in Riverside; and I was in Oberlin.

It was September, 1944; I was eighteen, when Mother and Dad finally arrived back in the States, essentially the end of their missionary career. It had been over four years since Dan and Warren had seen them; Dick and I hadn't seen Dad more than twice since he left us half way across China in 1940. And Dick and I had not seen Mom since she had left us in Renshow to join Dad in Southeast China.

It was reunion time. Mother's dream was to have the family back together, and Dad's dream to have a "house on the water." That meant not settling in his native Ohio, with its frigid winters, but heading for a milder climate in the Pacific Northwest.

Mom collected Dick and Warny and headed for Washington in a 1938 Ford sedan.

Mom, indefatigably optimistic, was ready to start over – for the umpteenth time. Every home she had ever established had been wiped out one way or another. A new home away from turmoil must have seemed like heaven on earth waiting for her.

After Dad had some business to take care of with the Mission Board, and I was through at Oberlin, we boarded the Northern Pacific Railway train and steamed west to catch up with the others.

Mom and the boys had already picked out a couple of likely houses around Ferndale, but Dad would have nothing to do with them. "Here, let me get my hands on that steering wheel. We are going to find a house on the water!"

By now with five of us piled in the car it was quite a merry ride. Dad would find a road along the water and follow it till it bent inland. Then he would go looking for another waterfront. It didn't take long to discover Drayton Harbor Road, which ran around the edges of a sheltered salt water harbor; Blaine and the Peace Arch into Canada on the north side and old farms on the south.

A hopeless looking hand written sign that might have been nailed to the fence post for several years, practically wailed at us: FARM 4 SALE.

Right across the road was a steep drop-off bank to the beach, just what Dad had longed for. "This is it!"

The farm had 23 acres, a neglected orchard, an adequate house, a dinky garage, a workshop, woodshed, and a big old barn a hundred yards or so up the hill.

Mr. Van Luven probably never really expected to sell his place, so he priced it at an exorbitant six thousand dollars. I doubt there was any dickering because Dad bought it on the spot. But the neighbors shook their heads. That Mr. Van Luven sure did pull a fast one on Reverend Terry -- imagine six thousand dollars for that old dump!

The big problem was that Mr. Van Luven didn't really want to move, either. The contract, whatever it was back then, gave him time to vacate but he made no signs of doing so. In the meantime, for several weeks we rented a cottage at Birch Bay. That was until Dad took matters in his own hands, went over and gave Mr. Van Luven a talking to.

It was typical Washington weather when we finally moved in, but one day the sky cleared, and when Mom saw what was across the water she let out a whoop, "Praise the LORD! Look at THAT VIEW!"

There the heavens declared to her the glory of God! The magnificent snow covered mountains north of Vancouver – hers to behold forever and ever -- a million dollar view that nobody could block. And Dad made sure that nothing ever blocked it. Off with the head of any tree down the bank that had the audacity to raise itself above the level of the road!

The house was built in 1903 of rock- solid virgin lumber, wide and thick. It was originally the headquarters of Drayton Harbor Oyster Company. Even though the company was gone, the oysters were still in great abundance, so thick one couldn't walk out without stepping on them at low tide.

Though the house looked small, ten foot ceilings gave it a roomy feeling. The living room and front bedroom looked out over the Harbor; the dining room, kitchen and bathroom were in back. Up the middle of the house was a steep staircase to two bedrooms and attics under eaves. It is just the same today, except for some remodeling downstairs and the "little house" which was built for "little Grandma Terry" who lived with the folks a while before she died in 1968.

Since then the little house has had multiple use: prolonged visits from family members, renters off and on, an office for Grace Harbor Farms and even Harbor House Bed and Breakfast.

When we Terrys came to Blaine, Dick went to Blaine High School, I began looking for a college; Warny hung around long enough to hate milking the cow, and went back to Antioch -- a cow had seemed a good idea, sort of.

Since there was no Presbyterian church, the folks joined the First Congregational Church, which Dad said was closest to what he believed. He built a reputation as the retired missionary Reverend, which he enjoyed, and bought a sail boat in which they explored Puget Sound.

Mom started a Young Mothers group which met weekly. Some moms in Blaine have fond memories of the encouraging letters she wrote to them and the happy times they had together. She also signed up for a Norman Rockwell correspondence painting class and did a lot of quaint oil paintings that still show up in Blaine garage sales.

Over time the old barn was torn down, the 23 acres were divided and sold. Four new neighbors' homes left the folks' place on two thirds of an acre – plenty for them

Mom was 81 when she died, six weeks after having a stoke in 1977. Dad lived alone in his beloved house on the water, with his cat, till he died in 1980 — after years of heart trouble. He was 84 and had attributed his long life to "knowing what is wrong with me and taking good care of myself."

Jonni [my daughter] bought the house, which became a haven for her through a heart breaking divorce. She painted it blue, planted roses all over the place and put a white picket fence around the yard. For the gate she had a special sign made: "Thou hast enclosed me behind and before and laid thy right hand upon me." [Psalm 139:5]

Jonni changed her name to Grace when she married Tim Lukens, and the next year, 1998, I took back my maiden name: no longer Svensson, but Terry again.

Grace and Tim invited me to live with them on their first wedding anniversary! What a gift for me to be with family again. There I was, age 72, back in the upstairs bedroom with the exact same window-view I'd loved when I was 18. How Mom would have chuckled at what she called "The pretty ways of Providence." Thank You, Lord!"

The Terry Family Letters

In front of that window I set up my computer and began a project:

Little Grandma Terry had left an amazing legacy at the folks' place: all the letters they had written from China – everything she could put her hands on, she had collected, even letters that went to Mom's folks in Texas. Grace had sorted and filed them by years and at one time offered them to Western University Archives, but so far nothing had been done with them. Up till then they were all safely stored in the attic.

Mom had written "home" every Sunday; Dad's letters were less frequent, but all of them give us an amazing record of their years in China: 1925 to1944.

In 1999 I decided to transcribe those fragile pages for the family. It was a lot of work which turned out to be a treasure for all of us, complete with old pictures and maps, newspaper clippings, and even letters from Dan, Warren, Dick and me.

Sometimes I would come across an account that made me storm downstairs and spout off to Grace and Tim -- can you imagine that THEY (or HE) did THAT! Often I would discover details about things I didn't remember or know about. When I was all through there were twelve ring binders of *Terry Family Letters* for the record. It took me till 2003 to complete the job and I enjoyed doing it as much as I am enjoying *this* project.

Grace Harbor Farms

In 1999 when the country was priming for Y-2K, Grace and Tim bought two goats – just in case the world shut down when calendars rolled over to the year 2000..

So began another saga: goat farming.

By 2005 things had grown way beyond two goats. They were then a grade A dairy, a well established local business: now Grace Harbor Farms -- and badly needed to relocate. They found the ideal location, but it was hard for Grace to part with the folks' place because she loved it so much. For a while she hoped to keep both places. Then one morning, with the sunrise turning the Harbor gold and the snowcaps pink, the Lord asked her, "Are you willing to move over and let somebody else learn to worship Me here?"

"In a heart-beat!" she answered. You have to know Grace to understand that passing on her faith is number one priority in her life. And so the fate of old house rests in God's hands, vacant, and well cared for by the present owner.

The Folks' Place today

PART TWO

The Family

In the beginning He made them male and female, and for this reason a man shall leave his father and his mother and be joined to his wife, and the two shall become one flesh.
[Matthew 19:4-5]

The Rev. and Mrs. Myron Eugene Terry
Request your presence at the wedding of their daughter
Rebecca Jean
To Floyd Eugene Svensson
on Saturday the twenty-fourth of August, 1947
at four o'clock in the afternoon
First Congregational Church
Blaine, Washington
Reception Following

Learning about Sex

If my mother were alive today, she would be one hundred and fifteen years old. She was a grand lady in every way possible: faithful and true to her husband and children, wonderfully gifted with a sense of humor, always optimistic, absolutely trusting the Lord Jesus Christ through incredibly difficult circumstances. I'm grateful to be her daughter. But she never taught me about sex.

Mom and Dad were born in 1895, in what we now call the Victorian Era. It was a time of great progress and change under the reign of Queen Victoria, from 1837 to 1901. Though she reigned in England, the era affected the US too: grand homes, elegant manners, and taboos which now seem prudish.

Coming out of that era, which influenced their upbringing, my parents passed on much of that to me. Sex, for instance, was never mentioned; in fact the word itself embarrassed me so much that I could barely say the word. Boys' and girls' anatomy had no names. My brothers had "that thing" which I didn't have; it was something I never thought to question or dared ask about, especially after I had that "terrible spanking" when I was little. Even through my teens I couldn't say "pants" -- it was more prudent to say "trousers."

The boys in the Canadian school wore such short shorts in the summer that I was embarrassed to look at them. -- Imagine that today, when girls and boys wear as little as possible – have you walked past the "strings" in Wal-Mart lately?

Unfortunately my sex education came in bumps. One summer night when I was ten, my brother Danny who was sixteen came to where I was sleeping and wanted to put "that thing" into me. I was flattered that he noticed me and tried to help him. "Are you sure that is the right place?" I asked. He said it was, but it wouldn't work. He tried another night, also to no avail, and then gave up.

That incident is mild compared to what other children have suffered. I didn't suffer, but I was afraid and ashamed. I never mentioned it to anyone and it put a barrier between Dan and me that lasted our whole lives.

Dan died on a merchant ship when he was 60; I was 54. His death devastated me, not because I missed him or grieved for him, but because there was unfinished business, something that never had been resolved or could be resolved between us. I was able to forgive him, between God and me, but not between us. My grief was for the loss of a brother who could have been my friend but never was.

I am grateful for the wonderful Canadian School in West China where I had my three first years of high school. There were no modern conveniences, but thoroughly good times every day.

When I arrived in mid term Bill Hibbard had decided, beforehand, that I was to be his girlfriend. At 14 this was quite a wonder to me. However, his idea of a date was walking around the yard with his head bent down resting on the top of my head -- hardly threatening. That was about all there was to being his girlfriend till he invited me to Canada in 2005 to replace his wife, who'd recently died. Well, Bill had no more attraction for me than he had 64 years earlier and I cut short the visit with no regrets.

The first and only time I was kissed in high school was in a play. The plot called for a kiss but Auntie Constance, our director, put Frank Price and me through a great deal of practice to pose in such a way that it looked like a kiss, but wasn't. On the night of the performance Frank grabbed me (not in the script) and planted a real one right in my face. I nearly panicked in surprise!

After my long trip back to the States, I finished high school at Riverside-Brookfield: another matter all together. Our graduation party ended up in pitch dark with the girls sitting on the boys' laps -- lots of giggling, wiggling and squirming, and...what? I left before I knew what else.

Another bump came on a camp-out with Westminster House – the Presbyterian club at UW. One of the leaders, Pastor X, who must have had a perverted sense of obligation to teach this little missionary kid the facts of life, invited me for a walk. Unsuspecting his motives, I went with him into the woods where he suggested we sit on log. There in very graphic detail he explained sex to me, so much so I began to be frightened by the way he looked at me. I suddenly had a flash back to Shanghai, when I was twelve. I had taken my cat to the vet and while we were supposedly waiting for the cat, the vet exposed himself and scared me half to death. Was that going to happen again! All I could think was, I have to get away from _this_ man. I can't remember how I got away without his touching me, but thank God I did.

I have to say I'm really glad that when Floyd and I were engaged Mom did talk to me. (She must have known that we were doing a lot of necking.) She took me into her bedroom, shut the door and told me that my Aunt T, Dad's sister, had a son out of wedlock [in the 1920's] before she married Uncle Percy. This was a FAMILY SECRET.

Dad was so shamed and upset over this scandal that Mom doubted he had ever gotten over it. Aunt T had kept it secret herself until almost the day she went into labor; and when Keith was born Aunt T's mother, little Grandma Terry, whisked him off that very night to a cousin who already had a bunch of kids. Thereafter nobody ever spoke of it, and though I knew my cousin Keith, I would never have guessed he was Aunt T's son.

As Mom shared the *secret*, I was petrified of "going too far." If that happened to me I'd never in the world be able to face my dad. I never mentioned the secret to Floyd, but thankfully, he had already told me that even in the Navy when all the sailors piled ashore to look for girls, he had never done so and wouldn't have sex till we were married.

Our wedding night was the first "going all the way" for both of us. I found out: being married is very good!

The Double Date

I met "Ole" Svensson on a double date when I was a junior at the University of Washington. He had taken pity on his roommate, Earl Oliver, who he claimed had no social life at all, and told him to ask somebody out. Earl knew me slightly and invited me. – You never know what slight acquaintances might lead you to!

Ole packed his date, who I can't remember in the slightest detail, Earl, and me into his black Dodge coupe, and we drove way north on Aurora Avenue to a sort of night club where there was dancing. About all I remember of that night was dancing with Ole, his smile, and the feel of his rough tweed coat.

The next day he called me up and asked to meet me for lunch. In the meantime he had asked Earl's permission — well, sure, Earl had said, anyway he hardly knew me. When we met at the cafeteria, Ole asked me to call him Floyd because that was his real name and he didn't want me to call him Ole for the rest of his life; which I didn't.

Floyd had started as a freshman at UW, then joined the Navy and was transferred to the "One Hundred Day Wonder" naval officer training at Columbia University, New York. Then after serving in the Philippines, returned as Ensign Svensson to UW for a master's degree in chemical engineering.

As for me, I had changed my major from English to "The Home." Floyd claimed that when I invited him to my cooking class and served him my apple pie, he was sunk.

Back in my secret attic, I always pictured a tall, dark and handsome prince who would sweep me off my feet and carry me up a circular staircase like Rhett Butler carried Scarlet, but Floyd was just the opposite, blonde and slight. The first time we went swimming and I saw his skinny legs I was really quite disappointed. Little did I know that those legs belonged to a future national champion in three countries at once!

Six months after the double date and a day after Floyd received his MS degree, we vowed "till death do us part" with Dad presiding and Mom playing the piano. Floyd was twenty-four, I was twenty-one -- and so began the Svensson family saga.

Naming Kids

Back in my secret attic I used to write stories about the family with ten kids. I don't remember any of the plots, if there were any. Maybe they all lived together in a cozy little house where you wouldn't be scared at night when all the lights were out! What I remember as the most important thing was selecting names: Geraldine, Josephine, Jacqueline, Roberta, promptly nicknamed, Gerry, Jo, Jackie, and Bobbie. All the girls had to have boy's names, and then they did many heck-of-a-swell things.

It may have been the logical conclusion to that dreaming what the rest of my life would be like. --- Well, here is the rest of the story:

Jonni, Christy, Janie, Eric, Nora and David

Until January 22nd, 1949, in Aberdeen, Washington, we didn't know whether "Watermelon" was to be a boy or a girl. Floyd was certain that the sex of a child depended on the strongest parent and therefore the first born would be a boy. Much to his surprise she turned out not to be one. But being so sold on the idea of boys being superior to girls, since I had decided back when I was ten that girls should have boy's names I naturally had the brilliant idea of naming her Jonnie Ann-- for Floyd's parents, John and Annie. Move the *ie* off Annie and add it to John. I thought it was really cute. Floyd hadn't given girl's names much thought and left it up to me.

A wise man said, "The future is written one day at a time by the choices you make today." I was a very naïve mother!

Little did I realize what a problem her name would be. Even though she changed it to Jonni in high school, her name had become a burdensome environment that she lived in. She was always asked, "Were you supposed to be a boy?" As a child she didn't know – so she tried to be a boy. It wasn't until many years later that she realized how hard she had tried to compensate for her name, and at age 50 she changed it to Grace Gloria —and that's a different story.

On April 12th, 1950, in Aberdeen another girl showed up. Floyd had no more to say about his strongest parent theory (nor did I!) I carefully chose a very feminine name, Christine Elaine.

On June 4th, 1951, as Ensign Svensson sailed out under the Golden Gate Bridge for Korea, Gloria Jane was born in Bellingham. It wasn't long before we called her Janie.

Floyd met her for the first time eleven months later. Now, Lieutenant JG Svensson, the confident naval officer, informed me he'd heard that we didn't need to use a diaphragm for birth control because there was a certain jell that worked. As a result on July 8th, 1953, he produced a boy!

Together we decided on a good Swedish name, Eric, to go with Svensson. Floyd felt like a king, and I was redeemed.

When Eric was born in Oakland, we were well established as part of the Junior College in Pleasant Hill, California. There were only 23 faculty members; we were all like family. The day Floyd was to bring Eric and me home from the hospital, the president's wife offered to take care of the other kids. That morning in order to get back for class on time, he hurriedly piled the girls, 4, 3, and 2, into the car, rushed over to the Buffingtons,' deposited them on the front steps, and took off. The only catch was that the houses in Sherman Acres all looked alike and he'd dropped them off at the wrong one before the astonished lady at the door bell could catch her breath.

Well, they got that sorted out, Floyd didn't lose his job, and life went on with normal Svensson chaos.

Quite unexpectedly, I got pregnant again: whew, number five on the way! On December 7th, 1959, Nora was born in Walnut Creek. I found her name on a paper napkin, printed all over with Swedish names, at a party we'd attended.

At one point Floyd's mother told us she hoped people would remember her maiden name, so we planned to use it for a boy or a girl's middle name, hence Nora Nylund Svensson. While I was pregnant we moved to Orinda.

"Another girl!" Eric groaned. He was six, and being out-numbered by four sisters was not something he looked forward to.

Jonni was 13 when I told her I was expecting again. She was totally shocked. "You're having another!" as though it was embarrassing and I was too old. Truthfully, I agreed: I thought I'd had enough.

On January 8th, 1963, David was born in Walnut Creek. We named him after his great uncle David, who was the first Svensson to migrate from Sweden just before World War One. At first I thought his middle name should be Terry, but then changed my mind and named him David Floyd. Of course, his dad had no objections to that.

Recently I have heard about parents who waited a few days after the baby arrived, taking time to get acquainted and to ask the Lord what name He would choose. It's a lovely idea, since children are a gift from God. But it never would have occurred to me to listen back then or to ask God about naming a child.

The Svensson family 1963
Christy, Floyd with Nora, Becky with David
Jonni in back, Janie far right, and Eric in front

Footnote: The Svensson stats now:

Floyd died in 2009 after a few years in a nursing home. He was 87.

Jonni, now Grace, married Bob Dolan and had Jasona and Heather. Now she is married to Tim Lukens who has sons Seth and David. She has five grandchildren.

Christy had Rachel, Robynne, Audra, Mark, and Davy, when she married Pete Rutherford. They have Nathan, Karen, DJ [Daniel John], Ryan, Laura, and Alex. Pete adopted the five kids from her previous two marriages, then added six more – eleven altogether.
Christy has twelve grandchildren and one great grand child.

Janie married Alan Ichikawa and had Jonathan and Anna. She died in 1986. Anna's three boys are her grandchildren. [Story to follow.]

Eric married Marlene Mirigian and they have Josh, Elliot, and Isaac. They have two daughters-in-law and a grandchild on the way.

Nora married John Mackey. They had Lauren. In 1983 John killed them both, then committed suicide. [Story to follow.]

David married Traute Christine Wallrichs and they have Sarah and Daniel.

As of today there are twenty one grandchildren, twenty one great grandchildren, and one great great granddaughter.

God, help me be a praying grandmother!

[I have refrained from telling the kids' own stories; I'll leave that up to them. I thank God for each of them; they are all amazing and precious to me in countless ways.]

The Champ

Part of Floyd's job was coaching the college tennis team. His love of tennis led to other racquet sports and one day he discovered squash. The speed and precision of that sport caught his fancy as nothing else had. Before long he was winning tournaments left and right, and became US national champ in the over forty category. That was quickly followed by winning the same titles in Canada and Mexico. "A tiger on the courts" his opponents applauded. I attended as many matches as I could and cheered him on. Once in a while things didn't go his way. I'll never forget the night we arrived for a match in Anaheim and who should show up as his opponent but a woman! He was so incensed I think he lost the match.

Sometimes his priorities were misplaced and painful for me. In 1963 he couldn't stick around while I was in labor with David because he had to be at a tournament someplace or other. When David was baptized he dropped into church just long enough to have him sprinkled, then took off for a match. On our twenty-fifth wedding anniversary he presented _me_ with.... a squash racquet, the funny old guy!

It wasn't long before he discovered racquetball and soon enjoyed the same winning streaks he had in squash.

I suppose every match had its own story, every opponent his own anecdotes about the champ, but I'll leave it at that because squash and racquet ball turned into building courts and clubs and all sorts of other entanglements from then on.

Cheerio! On with the story...

I Can Believe!

The disadvantage of having been a good girl all my life was the thick coating of goodness that prevented me from seeing reality. Hadn't I often listed to myself my wonderful attributes? Married to a genius college instructor, raised six brilliant children, became a respected Realtor, acquired much property, lived at 33 Sleepy Hollow Lane in prestigious Orinda, traveled the world, and so on and so on -- I drove a Mercedes even. Besides, I had so much _experience_.

Yet, something had gone so wrong that one day when Nora had come home from school very excited about something – can't remember good or bad – I couldn't even rejoice or grieve with her – whichever was required. I disappeared into the bedroom, and looking miserably out the huge window, blurted out, "What's wrong with me? I can't _feel_ anything?"

Five of the kids became Christians before I did. Janie was first and over the next few years was instrumental in Eric's, Nora's, and David's salvation. They were baptized, attended church regularly, had prayer meetings and Bible Studies in our living room; Young Life meetings there too.

Janie taught in a Christian school then transferred to Afghanistan to teach there. She was asked to leave after her second year for fear her vibrant witnessing to the Afghans would cause trouble for the school and/ or her arrest.

Eric spent a summer in Europe with Operation Mobilization. In 1973 he went on an extended mission trip to Ethiopia. I even went there to see him -- with the result, I'm sure, that those precious missionaries added their prayers to Eric's for my salvation.

I'd shake my head; they are SO *fundamental*, it's embarrassing. And to myself (I hope only to myself) I'd say, "Don't tell me about Christianity. I've been where the action is!" Meaning, of course, that because I was born on the mission field that covered everything. End of discussion

The kids were praying and working on me: "But, Mom," Nora, said "The Bible is the Word of God." Oh, yes, but not the only word, I'd say, or some other put down. Still I was just hanging on to my good old self. However, I was searching. There didn't seem to be answers for me at the Community Church where David had refused to go to Sunday school because "all they do is give you a box of crayons."

I plowed through books in that church's skimpy library and went to a few dreary Bible studies where the preacher seemed to spend his time asking us how we would explain feeding the 5,000 or some other miracle. Miracles were out, obviously, and prayer was discouraged because it "could get too personal." I experimented with automatic writing, visited the Mormon church, read self-help books, even some occult -- just about everything anyone suggested besides the Bible.

In 1976 Eric married Marlene. Jonni came from Alaska for the wedding and went back with enough curiosity and information to soon after give her heart to Jesus.

I ended up with a book Eric's mother-in-law, Gloria, handed me: *Something More*, by Catherine Marshall. I read it with great interest because here was an obviously well educated woman who believed that the Bible is the Word of God.

One of the chapters that impressed me most was her discussion of the Holy Spirit and the unholy spirit -- an entirely new concept for me. No one I knew talked about the Holy Spirit, and that the devil might be an unholy spirit clicked in my head. Something worth more investigation.

She had cross references and bibliography which I decided to check out. By the end of summer I realized I did in fact need to be born again -- well not because I was a sinner exactly [I realized that later] but because something was missing in my life – I wanted to *feel* again; I wanted the personal relationship with Jesus and peace like the kids had.

I was fifty years old when I invited Jesus into my heart. I started attending Fair Oaks, the kids' church, and for the first time in my memory herd a pastor-teacher go line by line through scripture, explaining what it meant and how it applied to me. A few months later I was baptized.

That good girl now had to be washed and rewashed in the blood of Jesus. I was not only the fastest, smartest, best at everything person I knew, but also the least humble and the most spiritual -- too much so to consider working in the church nursery, for instance.

Being born again was barely the beginning, like a naked baby, I had a lot of growing ahead.

I discovered the Bible Book Store and began reading just about everything, but still only a little of the Bible. When I found a book, *Prison to Praise* by Merlin Carothers, I was intrigued by his stories of praise in all situations.

Then he talked about speaking in tongues -- even now-a-days. I'd never heard of that! As far as I knew it had never happened again after the book of Acts. Yet I was fascinated; I thought if this is true that sounds like something I'd like to do.

Late one night, all alone in the living room, I asked God to give me the gift of tongues. "Just try it," I heard. So I made a couple of odd noises, and the next thing I knew a strange language poured out!

Oh! Oh, my goodness! I could hardly believe what was happening! What an incredible thing! Oh, God, I CAN believe! I CAN BELIEVE! I cried. The Bible is TRUE! The Bible is TRUE! I could speak words I couldn't understand, a language I'd never heard and I could do it whenever I wanted to -- amazing.

I was genuinely set free from all my doubts, my self-righteous sorting and discarding to pick out the truth. I started reading the Bible for all it's worth – that is no empty statement – it is ALL that is worth!

Jesus is God, and He is my Savior. More than that, He said he would send the Holy Spirit who would lead us in all truth; it is the Holy Spirit who directs my prayers and even gave me a different language to pray when I don't know how to pray. All of this is right there in the Bible! Fantastic!

The Bible IS the Word of God; it is the Truth, the Way and the Life.

I was in a kind of euphoria for months after. Nobody could tell me that Jesus isn't the only answer to everything I ever want or need.

I was a new creature in Christ -- still a baby, but a new one, born again!

Hallelujah!

PART THREE

The House on the Sand

Everyone who hears these sayings of mine and does not do them, will be like a foolish man who built his house on the sand: and when the rains fell, and the floods came, and the winds blew and beat against this house and it fell, and great was the fall of it. [Matthew 7:25-26]

Projects Ahoy!

In 1947 when we started planning our life together, Floyd wanted an army jeep in the worst way, but we settled for a 1932 Model A he heard was rusting away in somebody's back pasture. They wanted only $10 for it, so he bought it and dragged it to Tacoma where his mom re-upholstered the inside with canvas, even putting a zipper compartment overhead for a radio. Floyd spray painted it grey, got the engine running, found new tires, and—Eureka!—we had our honeymoon chariot.

We drove it all the way to California, via Highway 1, roasting corn-in-the-husk under the hood and sharing one sleeping bag at night.

A job interview in Antioch was disappointing—not that working for Dow Chemical wasn't attractive—but because the landscape was more like a desert and the dinky tract houses had no trees at all.

So much for California: back to Washington.

Aberdeen, Washington

Floyd was hired to teach chemistry at Gray's Harbor College in Aberdeen, where his salary was $3200 a year. We bought our first house for $1800; the $500 down payment was a gift from the estate of Grandma Collins' (Mother's mother.) Our monthly payment was $28.00. I got a job with the Singer Sewing Machine store and earned $26.00 a week. We felt very well off.

Now began **PROJECTS**: They progressed on a scale of zero up to...up to... well, up like an air balloon that took off and never came back down

Well, before I get into that I might mention that the first thing I bought was a band saw. I was really into wood working and set it up in the attic room to make kids toys and such. It was great fun. However, about six weeks into being Becky Svensson I figured out I needed a broom. Hmm. Time to think about housekeeping, I guess!

Floyd bought a Willys-Knight to refurbish, a sleeve valve roadster, collector's treasure, obsolete even then, but eventually abandoned in the weeds out back.

As for the Model A, it too ended up out back and was finally recycled for the second time to a student -- for $25-- which he never got around to paying. I wasn't all that happy with it anymore because it often sputtered dead from rust in the gas tank. In that model the tank was in front of the windshield on top of the engine; to reach across to the hood, uncap it, and reach down inside with a long wire, look down inside and try to push the rust chunks off the screen-covered feed hole --- well, I had to practically lie on the hood, which wasn't my favorite occupation – especially when pregnant.

Floyd had mild success resilvering mirrors. It was an easy sell to walk into a restaurant or bar, examine their scared-up mirror and talk the owner into having it jazzed up.

When we rented our house and bundled off to California after Floyd was called in for the Korean War, he stored several cases of wind-up fire alarms, which he'd been pedaling, in the attic – they'd have to wait till we were home again. One day in San Diego I got a call from our very irritated tenant: "There is a terrible commotion in the attic!" she yelled, "What am I supposed to do?" It had been a petty hot day, for Aberdeen, and all the alarms were going off at once!

#178 High Street, Pacheco, Martinez, California

After Korea, Floyd heard of a new junior college in Pleasant Hill, California, so he applied and was accepted at West Contra Costa Junior College [now Diablo Valley College.] We packed up, and in 1952 ended up in California after all.

Most of the teachers bought tract houses for about $6500, but that seemed too pricy for us, so we bought a little house in Pacheco, the small town near the college.

The next project was to remodel the house, which Floyd took on with a vengeance. He added a living room in front, three tiny bedrooms and a bathroom -- with a tub -- in back, and finally a huge cement slab sort of sun room on the side: i.e. the "smash court" with a back wall for batting balls against. Oh yes, and a fireplace in the living room because he'd picked up masonry on the side.

What else? It ended up a mish mash of a house, leaving one room with no more windows. I can't remember if the garage was there when we bought the place but I remember going into it a few weeks after Eric was born, dragging out the garbage can and smashing seven or eight dozen fruit jars into the can. I'll be darned, I thought, I don't have to can anything any more because...we have a freezer! Smashing glass was very satisfying.

Swifty's TV

Floyd was fascinated with TV from its inception. It was taking off like wildfire in the fifties and he was a natural to jump into the act, install antennas, fix and repair sets -- big box furniture with tubes in those days.

He even recruited me at various times to balance an antenna on the roof. The end of my cooperation in Antenna Holding was when I was eight months pregnant with Eric.

We had the first RCA color television in the county, other than a bar in Lafayette. That ranked us the most popular house in the neighborhood, needless to say, a gathering place for bunches of people to come and wonder at *color TV* ! Once when we lost the signal I had to call the bar to find out if their signal was lost too – it was.

House Moving

In the fifties the California Highway Department began to build a freeway from Walnut Creek to Oakland. This involved condemning all private homes in the way. Once they were owned by the State, open bidding was offered to anyone who wanted to buy and move them at their own expense.

The potential here really caught Floyd's fancy. Lots were cheap in Pacheco, so it was an ideal set-up for getting rich. I'll never forget the first house coming up High Street with Floyd sitting on the top like a sultan riding an elephant. He'd bid $7.00 and got it!

Third Ave South, Pacheco

He sent me to bid on the fourth house he moved: I bid $28.00 for him and we got that one; it was too good to pass up. It would be set down below the road — well, not exactly. He decided it must have a basement with three little bedrooms and with a fireplace with a barbeque, and a formal fireplace upstairs, and a circular driveway, and so forth because we'd move in ourselves. Unfortunately, Floyd wasn't really good at finishing projects, especially grand ones. The basement wasn't really finished and wasn't really right and when his mother came to visit the first time and slept in the basement, unfortunately that particular night it rained and she was stranded in several inches of water.

The asparagus sorting machine

This was a brilliant invention that shot all sizes of asparagus down a shoot with various sized holes for it to fall through. I never actually saw it, and he never built it, but he explained the design to somebody somewhere who picked up the idea and used it. We had a lot of fun kidding him about it, but it never earned him a buck.

Becky to the rescue

I was beginning to think it would be a good idea if I had a supplementary income, especially since my last venture to sew any dress you want for five dollars ["You supply the pattern and material"] had done me in after a customer ordered 8 princess-style red velveteen bridesmaids dresses for her daughter's wedding.

Maybe I could sell real estate. Floyd thought that was a great idea because it would give us access to all sorts of potential projects. So I got a license and spent boring hours waiting for buyers in an office or on a tract. That wasn't any fun at al and produced virtually no income.

So, I decided I'd finish my education and be a teacher; should work, then I'd have summers off with the family. I enrolled in UC Berkeley, but half way thru the semester I got pregnant, with Nora. Floyd teased that if I hadn't done so poorly in statistics and gotten a "C", I wouldn't have gotten pregnant! Anyway, so much for college till another time.

8 Alta Vista, Orinda, California

I was still getting information from Multiple Listing and one listing caught my eye: Orinda home in the hills, only $12,000. We gotta see it, said Floyd, and we did, bought it for $10,000, and moved to Orinda.

Many parts of Orinda had been severely affected by mud slides, and many houses had been abandoned and / or condemned. Our property had been damaged only by the collapse of part of the driveway, so was quite a "deal" for us.

Moving day was crazy because five or six of Floyd's fellow teachers came to help. As they were packing stuff into miscellaneous pick-up trucks one of them asked me where Floyd was. I had to tell them he wasn't there because he was playing in a tennis match. Oops! I couldn't cover for him, and hoped they would give him a REAL bad time when he showed up for classes on Monday.

Alta Vista, a small road off the top of El Toyonal, is a quick shot over Grizzly Peak to Berkeley. Our house was way down below the road where it couldn't be seen from the road.

The driveway was up past the mailbox around a sharp U turn and back down to the house. The house was surrounded by trees and quite dark inside. By the time we moved on to the next project we had 6 kids and Floyd had added a living room on one end, a master bedroom on the other end, and a few other improvements that never got finished.

Orinda is the first town through the tunnel from the Oakland-Berkeley Hills. In real estate terms, it was considered the elite residential address where the property values were higher than farther away from the city – meaning San Francisco. Of course that made it seem attractive to Floyd and me, notwithstanding that on El Toyonal there were many small homes, some of them old summer cottages. There was one of those near us that had only a mud floor.

Around us were families like our own, kids riding the school bus together, and friends for me. I joined a baby-sitting co-op where we took turns sitting for each other and I discovered that they had the same kinds of cold cereal in their cupboards that we had. Being prestigious was no different than being just ordinary folks.

A tennis court

Between the house and the beginning of the driveway our land extended far enough for – Floyd figured – another house and a tennis court. A tennis court on this down slope? Are you kidding? Of course not kidding. Two slide-damaged houses up the road could be salvaged for concrete to build a retaining wall – and Voila! a full-size court! No matter if he didn't get around to a fence; he knew where he could pick up old gill nets, which he draped around to keep the balls in.

He thought his kids should learn to play tennis but that was hopeless. When I made a tennis dress for Jonni, she was 14, and nearly puked—horses were her thing. But I learned to play and really enjoyed the game; even though I wasn't very good, I made some great friends.

#10 Alta Vista -- unfortunately...

As for building a house next door, when David was a couple of weeks old it was in full progress. The front door was in the middle of three floors, the kids' bedrooms down, ours up – a good design for the severe down-slope lot.

One day the lone worker came over to get me – "They're delivering concrete, and there's too much wet cement and I don't know what to do about it!" (As though I did!)

I put David in the car and raced down to the hardware store for buckets and shovels. A second load of cement was delivered by mix-up and the house ended up with double retaining walls a few feet apart, one inside the other.

The septic tank was to be in the small level spot adjacent the foundation. When it was partly dug out the guy who came to finish the job fell into the hole, bulldozer and all. That required a monster crane to pull him out -- just another day at the Svenssons.

December, 1963. One way or another, 10 Alta Vista was signed off by the building inspector and we moved in. Unfortunately, Floyd typically hadn't concerned himself with finishing things; details should take care of themselves. Unfortunately the linoleum was carelessly laid with the seams off center; the carpet wasn't laid at all, nor were there any baseboards. Floyd's brother Jack helped install the windows, and one in the living room was upside down. In our bedroom upstairs the exposed rafters and cross braces were slapped together any old way, nothing aligned or straight. Outside, the concrete driveway was poured right up to the front step, leaving not a square foot to plant a geranium.

I can't say I exactly hated the place, even though it was roomy enough for us all, but I was gravely disappointed. I groaned because even the siding Floyd had chosen, battleship grey, looked so ugly -- unfortunately.

The Insulation Caper

1966: This one I can hardly describe because it came and went so quickly. Floyd took over a company in Redwood City that was making insulation out of newspaper pulp. This would require a long commute from college, through the tunnel to Oakland, down the freeway, across the bridge to the San Francisco peninsula, and back to Orinda. Just about then Christy declared that she couldn't stand Miramonte High School. Now, I take the blame here, because I thought we should move to San Leandro which would solve Floyd's commute and Christy' dilemma -- which we did. But by the time we were barely settled, the whole manufacturing idea somehow evaporated and it seemed only sensible to move back to Orinda.

#2 Camino Del Monte, Orinda

1967: Because we had rented 10 Alta Vista, we moved into the little house at the top of our old driveway. It was abandoned, but on close examination, only one side was wrecked, so Floyd simply sawed it in half, raised the damaged side, put it on a new foundation, attached it back to the good part with a couple of steps in between levels. And –yep! another house.

We moved into that till the renters moved out and we could have #10 back again. Christy, Janie, and Eric finished their school year in San Leandro by a daily commute – Christy driving. [Jonni was in Blaine with the grandparents for her senior year in high school, and married Bob Dolan in December, 1967.].

#33 Sleepy Hollow Lane, Orinda

1969: I was a full time real estate agent, and one night told Floyd about a big slide-damaged house I had toured in Sleepy Hollow, on the other side of Orinda. The slab floor in the 22 foot living room sloped nine inches from one side to the other. [I measured it myself.] That is why the Svenssons were able to buy the place– all 3600 square feet of it – for only $32,000.

In spite of the tilt it was a great house for us, radiant heat, plenty of room, and walking distance to Sleepy Hollow School, where Nora and David were in the third and first grades. And it wasn't long before Floyd had tucked a full sized squash court into the hill behind us—almost completely finished except open to the air above the back wall. We lived there longer than any other house – twelve years.

#32 Sleepy Hollow Lane

The lot across the street was damaged by the same slide that had tilted the floors of our house. It was condemned for building, but was for sale, cheap. Floyd bought it and designed a house that sat on more than twenty reinforced cement piers, each 28 feet deep. Thus he got a building permit and built it Spanish style, with a tile roof and arched portico entry. When we sold it a bit later, he kindly threw in a tennis court on the back of the lot, which was unfortunate because the new owners sued him when it started to break apart. [The last I heard the place was sold for $2,300,000!]

Bellingham, a simpler life...?

Floyd liked to "get away" to Reno; he could play tennis, poker, and crash with TV in a hotel room. Often I tagged along, though I didn't enjoy it. Driving home from an unhappy weekend I told him how futile and irrelevant our life was becoming. We had no relationship with each other any more — he was absorbed in his stuff and I was left wandering aimlessly around.

For a change he didn't belittle me but said he was dissatisfied too. How come I was always the one who took David shopping – how come I never asked him to go with David to get new shoes? I was flabbergasted. Never once had he ever suggested that he could take anybody shopping. We looked at each other as though we were just getting acquainted.

Before we got home from that escapade we had decided that maybe we should simplify our lives; sell our house, move to Bellingham and ... start over.

In 1978 we did move to Bellingham, David, Nora, dog and all. [The other kids were married or gone.] I was full of hope that we could pull it together, but hope for a simpler life flew out the window when Floyd wanted the biggest house in town: 158 South Forest Street: 13,000 square feet, five stories, ten bedrooms, seven bathrooms and a grand ballroom, built in 1903 for the mayor of Fairhaven. "Only $150,000!"

[That was during the time when I thought I should be a submissive wife, and raised no objections. I rationalized that we could rent rooms to college students. But, turned out it wasn't zoned that way and the neighbors were up in arms and some spiteful person on Halloween threw raw eggs at the kitchen window!]

Floyd's insatiable need to have <u>A Project</u> wasn't satisfied till he purchased the abandoned Carnation Milk plant in Mt.Vernon -- to convert to a racquet ball-community center. No, it didn't happen, but the chimney we owned for a few months is now painted like a tulip, and still towers over downtown Mt.Vernon.

Also he thought a yacht would be great recreation in his spare time and bought one for $48,000. As that idea turned out he had it on the water only three times, and always with the yacht salesman on board because he didn't know how it operated.

Floyd often told me that millionaires were made not by how much money they had in the bank, but how much they could borrow. He had a genuine charisma about him when it came to persuasion; he could persuade most anybody to do most anything when it came to an adventure, an investment or a new idea.

His charisma wasn't limited to individuals; it worked on banks and credit unions. When we bought the big house in Bellingham, and a yacht, and the Carnation plant in Mt Vernon, I'm sure the loan officers were convinced a millionaire had come to town.

158 So. Forest Street

Actually, David, Nora and I saw him only every other weekend because he still had too many projects going in the Bay Area and he had no intention, after all, of giving up teaching. Sometime during all this he purchased the Canyon Swim Club in El Sobrante and was quickly in the process of adding three or four racquet ball courts to the club.

We were in the Bellingham house only 7 months when we moved back to California. Instead of selling the yacht, he exchanged it for a smaller one, because obviously it would turn a hefty profit when he sold it in San Francisco. Also to not waste money on hiring a moving van to move us, he purchased a refrigerated truck --obviously a good investment for bringing fish down from Alaska -- someday.

Some caravan we were when we pulled onto I-5: A high white truck with refrigerated furniture pulling a yacht; bringing up the rear a white haired lady in a blue diesel Mercedes with an eager golden retriever flapping her ears out the window!

I don't remember what happened to the boat; the last time I saw it, it was stuck in the mud where Floyd had miscalculated backing up the truck and trailer somewhere in Oregon.

Fare-thee-well, simplified life ... Onward, backward, whatever ....

Back again at #33 Sleepy Hollow, life was fairly normal — well normal for Svenssons-- till Floyd decided it was time to level the floors and remodel the house. By now property values were such that he could borrow $150,000 on the house we bought for $32,000 only twelve years before. Also the idea was attractive since he'd just added a motor home to his conglomeration of might-come-in-handies. So with a sad okay I agreed to living in the motor home at the racquet club while the remodeling went on.

Of all the moves we made that was the worst – from more space than we could use to an old motor home --yieks! Not that I longed for a palace -- a simple little cottage would do-- but I suddenly found myself in a fish bowl inside a television set, or vise versa.

By fall, even though there was only a livable bedroom and bathroom, I insisted on going back to #33. Thus it was we now resided in #33 "Empty Hollow Lane!" I suppose I could have philosophized about that but I didn't think up the name till now.

Reflection
Sometimes these days when I lie awake thinking about the past I count properties. I think of each move we made, the houses we bought or fixed up or left unfinished. There were pieces of land, a manufacturing enterprise or two, some places I never even saw. I use my fingers under the covers, fives on my left hand, tens on my right, and by the time I'm past the twenties, I can't remember what fingers are what and lose track. It's too much for me; forget the numbers.... and I go to sleep.

In trying hard to be a good girl, to be agreeable, to give Floyd support, I didn't have the guts to say no or to challenge him -- in fact, I was afraid to.

If I wanted to present my case for putting sheetrock on the unfinished bedroom walls, for instance, I planned for days how I would word it, and looked for an appropriate time to talk. But I invariably met with an excuse or even a scolding. I didn't know how to get his attention and often ended up crying, which only made him more angry with me. So I just made the best of it and moved another lumber pile.

Floyd bought, collected, and misplaced pickup trucks, dump trucks, a refrigerator truck or two, bulldozers, a motor grader, a motor home, a camper trailer, more cars than I can remember.

If you are running out of breath, so am I! I'll not ride you up and down this roller coaster any more. I never did like roller coasters; ever since my first ride on a real one when I was little. I'd thought my stomach would fly out of me on the next drop, and who needs that?

The Crash, October, 1981

The Monday after we'd been to a Full Gospel Businessmen's' convention in Redding, where Floyd had bought a trailer park before breakfast, Jonni called from Blaine: "Listen to this, Mom," she said, and read me the description of manic depression. Everything suddenly clicked. I knew there was something crazy going on but had no idea what, only struggling to keep my balance. Right away I felt as though I had an iron rod in me, which I tightened up with both hands. I began drastic action. I went to the bank and closed our joint account – just moments before Floyd tried to draw everything out at another branch. A knowledgeable man who was working for us advised me: "You can't handle this alone; get the whole family together and have Floyd locked up."

Eric came from Toronto where they were working with an international disaster rescue mission -- little knowing rescue was needed at home! Jonni and Christy came from Washington and Oregon. Janie was expecting a baby any minute; she was nearby. Nora came from Berkeley where John was in school. David was the only one at home, first hand witness to the craziness

Jonni arrived first, and the next morning at 3:00 AM Floyd woke her up. "I'm ready to go!" He drove recklessly all over the Bay Area from one project or another, fully possessed by demons. He was screaming, yelling, or cussing, tape recording himself, not even slightly rational. Part way through the craziness they swung by the airport, picked up Eric, and continued to careen from one thing to another.

One stop was a video game company where he ordered 180 free-standing video game machines for the racquet ball club; another stop to order several manufactured homes he wanted delivered by helicopter to the club.

Afraid Floyd would become dangerously violent, Jonni tried as best she could to cancel everything with hand and eye signals, and hurried apologies -- if she could catch the wide-eyed salespeople -- before Floyd hurried them out again.

That evening when the whole family was gathered back in torn-apart number 33 where the windows were out and most of the furniture piled into the squash court —we sat around the table and confronted Floyd. We even had a police officer on call in case he got violent. But, thank God, he reluctantly agreed to get help. He limply let Eric and Jonni drive him to Kaiser Hospital psychiatric ward where they were waiting for him, but it wasn't all that easy. As soon as they got there he took off and ran. As Eric ran to the hospital for assistance, Jonni stopped Floyd in the parking lot and talked him into going with her to the hospital.

Janie and I had followed to the hospital, where he was "being evaluated," but by the time we got there they had put him a straight jacket, and were loading him into an ambulance. When he saw me he yelled, "I'm going to divorce you for this, Becky!"

The next afternoon, October 10, 1981, Janie delivered Jonathan Pablo Ichikawa. What a blessing, what a promise for a future to look forward to, God gives good gifts to his children!

The Wilderness

When we put Floyd in the hospital, 33 Sleepy Hollow was uninhabitable and about to be taken over by the bank. I enlisted my fellow broker, Lyman Lee, to find a rental in Pleasant Hill, near the college, and moved in before Floyd was released to come home. This was hard on David because he didn't understand why I was taking over and making decisions so fast. But a pastor friend of ours kindly explained it had to be that way as long as his dad couldn't be depended on.

After his first week, Floyd was granted permission to come home for the weekend. By Monday he seemed to be quite calm so I thought he could just stay home, and his doctor, though unsure, said okay. No telling if another week would have made any difference, and little did I suspect that the first lock-down wouldn't be the last -- not by any means -- nor that his illness would continue to escalate, exacerbated by alcohol, sleepless nights, and rage. Being diagnosed manic depressive seemed to give him permission to be everything he was meant to be – i.e. crazy!

How could I cope? Often I went for a bike ride in the neighborhood looking at other folks' homes where things seemed quite normal, at least from the outside. With some strange sense of community service, if I happened to see an abandoned grocery cart I would pull it back to the store, one hand on the handle bar, one on the cart -- anything to calm my soul.

I wondered if my life would ever be normal again. But what was normal? I was an emotional wreck.

More than once I went to stay with friends or family, but that didn't help much. It was impossible to explain to Floyd that I wasn't doing well; his response was "Boy, you sure aren't!"

In the spring of 1982 I threw some clothes, a sleeping bag, a little coffee maker, my sewing machine, my Bible, and my camera into my car. I didn't know what I had in mind, I was just going – just somewhere. Maybe all the way to Toronto where Eric and Marlene were expecting their second baby. Maybe I could help them... maybe, maybe.... but what shall I do?

I ended up at the Grand Canyon where I got a room in the lodge and called home. All I wanted to say is, "I'm okay, don't worry about me; I'm going to Toronto."

The next day I started the long walk along the Rim. Quite frequently I came across plaques set in the rocks, scriptures that reminded me this is God's amazing creation.

I came to an outcropping where someone had erected a small cross, not much taller than I. I stopped there a long time. Then I took off my coat, my shoes, whatever else I was carrying, and put it all on the rock at the foot the cross "I surrender, God; I give it all to you. You know where I have to go and what the future holds. I give up everything, Lord. Thank you for bringing me here."

As I continued my walk I heard "Read Hebrews 3: 7-13." I didn't know what it would say till I got back to the lodge, but it became my comfort and direction for the miles ahead.

"Just as the Holy Spirit says,
Today if you hear His voice,
Do not harden your hearts as when they provoked me,
As in the day of trial in the Wilderness,
When our fathers tried me by testing me,

And saw my works for forty years.
Therefore I was angry with this generation,
And said, 'They always go astray in their heart;
And they did not know my ways.
As I swore in my wrath,
They shall not enter my rest.'

"Take care, brethren, lest there should be in any of you an evil, unbelieving heart, in falling away from the living God.

"But encourage one another day after day, as long as it is still called 'Today' lest any one of you be hardened by the deceitfulness of sin."

More at peace, I continued driving till I was tired, often making coffee in a rest area; or I parked in a well-lighted all-night gas station and slept a few hours. Every day or so I would call home and report that I was okay.

On one of those calls from a rest stop Floyd said, "Where ARE you? You better call Eric because the baby was born and he might not make it!"

What was I supposed to do? As I closed the phone booth I noticed a man rummaging for something in the back of his pickup, the only person around. I went right over and said, "Pardon me, sir, are you a Christian? Will you pray with me?"

He looked startled, then said kindly, "Well sure. What is the problem?"

I explained that I just had a grandson and he wasn't doing very well. Maybe he wouldn't make it.

Right away the man looked stricken. "Oh, God!" he gasped, "that just happened to my daughter -- but her baby didn't make it!" He was suddenly all choked up.

My heart turned over. I grabbed his hands, "Then I have to pray for you!"

At that moment the Holy Spirit took over and prayed through me; prayed for him and his daughter, her mother and their whole family: comfort, peace and other things entirely not my words because at that moment I didn't know how to pray.

We were both crying. Then the dear man prayed that I would have peace, a safe trip, and that God would protect that little guy up in Toronto.

How amazing! God will take two of his children a long long way to be used for His purpose -- and time it just right for them to be in the right place at the right time!

Beyond ordering lunch or buying gas, that encounter was the only interaction I had with anybody on the whole trip.

I didn't make it directly to Toronto because I was half way across Ohio before I realized I'd missed the turnoff for Detroit. I ended up instead in Buffalo, where I lapped back and passed Niagara Falls on the way to Toronto. Grand Canyon to Niagara Falls –quite a trip!

When I finally got to Eric's mission station, Elliot Eric Edwin Svensson had passed the crisis, though he was still in the hospital with Marlene. My rattled arrival wasn't really any help to them: their small trailer had no place for me to sleep except on the floor, plus it was only a week before Floyd called and said that if I didn't come home right away he'd divorce me.

I knew I had to go back no matter what, so I headed home, maybe a little stronger, maybe a little more prepared; it wasn't over yet. I didn't want "to fall away from the living God" -- I prayed I'd hear His voice and believe; His rest still lay somewhere in the distance.

Nora and John

> Yeah, though I walk through the valley
> of the shadow of death,
> I will fear no evil; for Thou art with me;
> Thy rod, and Thy staff shall comfort me.
> [Psalm 23:4]

One day when Nora was reading her Bible in the college library, a taller than six foot young man with dark hair and a friendly smile approached her. "I see you are reading the Bible," he said. "I'd like to know more about it."

It was a perfect ploy to get her interest, and they struck up a conversation. One thing led to another, and even though she eventually had tried to avoid him, he persisted. We heard later that he had vowed that he was going to "get an Orinda girl pregnant," and... he succeeded

My mistake was in encouraging her to marry him. I should have known that getting married was not necessarily a solution to being pregnant. I doubt that was John's intention but nevertheless they married in Bellingham in the chapel of our big house.

The marriage was doomed to failure from the beginning. Nora realized that on their honeymoon, but she wasn't able or willing to admit it. She hoped she could be a witness to her friends that even though she'd made a mistake she would somehow right the wrong. She was only 19, and John 21 when Lauren Gold was born on May 11, 1979.

None of us realized that John was abusing Nora; she didn't want to tell anyone until three years into her marriage when Janie asked her about bruises on her arms and legs. When the truth came out she was too afraid to do anything but hurry back to John. [I have learned so much about abused wives— after the fact!]

Finally she decided to leave him. I helped her pack a few things and drove her and Lauren to Blaine for refuge with Jonni and Bob. But somehow John smooth-talked her into returning to California. He wouldn't give her a bad time, he would give her a divorce, he wanted to be a good dad for Lauren, and so forth.

When she came back, Floyd, David, and I had just moved into a small house in Pacheco. Hardly room for her and Lauren, so she rented a little garage apartment and went back to the waitress job she had left to go to Washington.

She had a bunch of friends help move -- even her piano -- into her apartment. Someone told me she was so happy she played the piano almost all night.

She had been back from Washington less than ten days when on her first weekend at her job she left Lauren with John, who was living with his dad, Jack Mackey, in his ramshackle old house on Danville Boulevard in Alamo. It seemed hopeful that she would get her life back on track.

About noon, on Monday May 2, 1983, I was driving down Danville Boulevard on my way to a friend's house for lunch, when I noticed white TV trucks, blinking police cars, and Jack's place taped off with yellow tape.

I stopped my car, got out, ducked under the tape, and was met by a tall police officer striding across the grass. Wanting him to know that I had a right to be there, I said, "My daughter is married to John Mackey, is there a problem here?"

Immediately sizing me up, he insisted I go back to my car where he opened the passenger door and sat me down. With the door open he crouched down to my eye level, and said, "Your daughter is dead and your granddaughter is dying."

Trembling, I said, "Are you sure?"

Yes, he was sure; John had beaten them with a pipe, part of his weight lifting equipment. Nora was dead and Lauren had been rushed to the hospital, where she was dying. John had screeched away in his car – they knew that much – but they didn't know where he was.

Somehow I managed to say, "Then I have to tell my family." I pulled out of my purse the little phone book I'd put together only a few days before.

The officer ushered me over to the daycare center across the street, which the police had emptied and borrowed for a command post, as Nora's body was still in Jack's house and the place was swarming with investigators.

As I reached one person after another the officer would take the phone and help me talk to them because I was crying so hard. I'd reached Jonni in Washington and Christy in Oregon, and they were flying down.

I'm convinced that hard as it was, it was not by chance that God brought me to Jack's house at that very hour, and it was only by His strength that I got through what I had come upon and had to do.

Pretty soon the small building was full of people: Floyd, Janie, Eric, David, our pastor, my Bible study leader, a few friends, and several police officers, collected together in the day care center.

Suddenly somebody announced, "We have to pray for John!" I was already so shaken I could barely stand. I CAN'T PRAY!! Yet people on each side grabbed my hands as they circled and started praying for John. I rolled my eyes toward the ceiling and cried "Oh, God, this is too much for me --You take care of John!"

Somehow we piled into our various cars and got home. Before the night was over our small living room was filled with weeping friends. Some said they would never trust God again; some were angry, more than one said they were glad that "John is in hell." Jonni held Nora's purse in her hands and wept and wept.

Next morning, imagine my shock when I went out to get the paper off the porch and there was my picture on the front page with the officer walking me across the grass. The headlines were full of the heinous double murder in Alamo.

The next day Jonni, Christy and several others went to Nora's apartment and gathered together some of her things. I didn't go, but someone brought her Bible and laid it on the dining room table.

Seeing it there, I flipped it open without picking it up. I had to have something from the Lord – anything! Suddenly it seemed alive, almost as though a beam of light from it was filling the room. I leaned over without touching it and read "No longer do I call you slaves; for the slave does not know what his master is doing; but I have called you friends, for all things that I have heard from My Father I have made known to you." [John 15:15]

What did that mean? What was God telling me? But immediately I was lost in a heavenly embrace -- that's the only way I can describe it. I felt as though I was sobbing against His heart, His arms surrounding me, His head leaning against mine, and He was weeping with me. "I too saw my son beaten to death," He said.

Incredibly I felt the power of God fill me; I felt so strong that if John had appeared at the door I was sure I could have said, "Drop dead in the name of Jesus!" and he would have.

My brother Warny showed up in such bad shape from a bad back he could barely get out of his car. I laid my hand on his back and said, "Be healed, in the name of Jesus," – and he was immediately pain free, straightened up and walked normally into the house!

My friend Mary Cummins came on her way to see the doctor for an eye infection. "Never mind the doctor," I said. "There is so much power here that God will heal your eye." So I touched her bright red eye: "God, please heal Mary's eye," and immediately the redness cleared and it was all well!

Awhile later I read the verses following: John 15:16:

"You did not choose Me, but I chose you, and appointed you, that you should go and bear fruit, and that your fruit should remain, that whatever you ask of the Father in My name, He may give to you."

Wow, I had seen it happen right before my eyes!

But in spite of that, to put it mildly, it was a horrible time. I likened it to the explosion of an atomic bomb: everybody was too torn apart to even look at the other damaged people lying around -- to do a thing to help each other.

And Floyd? If he wasn't melted into the TV, he would bang out the door in the middle of the night and run, sometimes twenty five miles; often he fumed at David or me, or even at Nora herself. The day after Nora and Lauren died the poor guy was sobbing at the kitchen table, head in hands. When I tried to talk to him he cried, "They are gone, and I don't even have enough money for a funeral."

What could I say? It was true.

I spent days wrapped in a scratchy old army blanket, lying on the couch, struggling with fatigue, guilt and accusing memories of Nora's life. -- O Lord, why didn't I pay attention when Nora said so and so; why didn't I discourage her from marrying John in the first place? Where was I when she needed me ......? And so on and on, accusations tormenting me.

Also I anguished that this would cause my kids to lose their faith in God. When I was praying about that the Lord asked me if I had released them to Him. Well, I guessed I had, hadn't I?

But then I heard, "Yes, but have you released them to unbelief?"

"No, of course not; I want them to believe in You!"

"Well think about this," I heard. "That is what I have done with everybody ever born. I have surrounded them with enough evidence of Who I am for them to choose Me of their own accord."

I was startled, to say the least, but coming to think about it, that is exactly what the Bible says, and at that I did release them. That in turn released *me* from a lot of unnecessary turmoil.

John committed suicide by driving his Honda at high speed off Grizzly Peak above UC Berkeley. The car hurtled 300 feet through the air, investigators estimated, to land in a thick grove of eucalyptus trees. His body was found by hikers on June 27th, my birthday, more than 8 weeks after he had disappeared.

During those terrible weeks we had a lot of interaction with John's parents Jack and Marilyn, who had been separated since John was three years old. Our mutual grief created a weird bond between us. When John's body was found I agreed to drive Marilyn to the Oakland morgue to identify it. Though the personnel were reluctant to show it to us, they went to the trouble of arranging it behind a plate glass viewing window. We could look at it only from behind a kind of rail a few feet away.

I won't describe it; believe me, a decaying body is a sight to turn your stomach.

After Marilyn identified what was left of a sweater, we silently headed home. She just stared out the window. So, that was it. But before I dropped her off I stopped at a florist and bought her a bouquet of flowers. There was nothing else I could do.

Sometime in the summer after a conversation with Marilyn who said she'd NEVER forgive John, I was surprised to realize that I held no hatred or bitterness toward John. I had hardly even thought about that when so much anger was raging around me.

It was a puzzle until I attended a Women's Aglow retreat. The speaker put us through an exercise of "searching our basements," as we all have unforgivenes stored in our hearts against people in our lives, junk that needs to be brought out and "nailed too the cross." It is a clear command of Jesus that if we don't forgive others their trespasses he cannot forgive us ours.

The women all prayed for God to show us who we held captive in our "basements;" who we needed to forgive. I went into mine and discovered three people there: my brother, my husband, and my dad.

The next step was to share with each other the names of people God had showed us and ask him to forgive them, and forgive _us_ for keeping them bound in our "basements" of unforgiveness.

I was amazed that John's name was not one on my list! How could that be, Lord, I asked?

"Remember when you asked Me to take care of John?"
"Yes, I do."
"Well, right then I took all the responsibility off you and carried it myself." Wow!

I was reminded that Jesus on the cross said, "Father, forgive them because they know not what they do." And Stephen, when he was being stoned, said, "Father, don't hold this sin against them." Both of them gave God the responsibility of forgiving those who put them to death.

"But, God," I said, "what about the seventy times seven bit?"

"Seventy times seven: those are your daily walking orders. When it comes to judgment, that is Mine."

Not only was I free from holding John captive, I learned how to let go of the guilty accusations I heaped on myself. Every time one of those big waves seemed about to knock me off the rock, I'd cry "O, Lord, forgive me!"

God doesn't have to call a committee meeting for times like that; he forgives on the spot. The wave would fall away, and I stood on the rock, forgiven, washed and clean.

His forgiveness is too sweet a thing to take lightly It is the heart of the Gospel, the passion of Jesus, a gift that cannot be ignored, neglected, or even understood. It truly is the gift that sets men free. O, thank God!

Nora and Lauren, April, 1983

Living with Insanity

"When an evil spirit comes out of a man, it goes through arid places seeking rest and does not find it. Then it says, 'I will return to the house I left.' and takes seven other spirits more wicked than itself, and they go in and live there. And then the final condition of that man is worst than the first." [Luke 11:24-26]

Floyd was always more manic than depressive; if he took lithium as he was supposed to, it kept him fairly normal. But none of that; he complained that normal was depressing, and refused to take it. Once in a while, though, he was depressed and would barely move off the couch.

Nothing was predictable. I could get a call day or night that he had been picked up by the police, even as far away as Monterey or Reno. The pattern was a 72-hour lock-down in a psychiatric ward in Oakland or Martinez. We knew we were dealing with at least one demon in Floyd. I believe that the day he "decided to be a Christian" and he raised his hands above his head and yelled out "I want it ALL," was the day that demons of the devil jumped in and said, "We got him!"

Why? Because he thought by declaring he was a Christian was all it took -- with no idea of asking Jesus to save him, no idea that he needed to repent for anything, just thinking it was a great way to get rich or join the crowd – God only knows – but in no way believing he was a sinner or making a commitment to Jesus Christ.

So he went his merry way.

When he went to church with me one time, I asked him if he would let the pastor pray for him. "Sure, I want all I can get."

The pastor, knowing what was needed, prayed for his deliverance from evil spirits, and Floyd declared he was free. But... as the Bible says, when the devil saw the house was clean -- if in fact it was-- he sent seven more demons worse than the first.

One day I met the demon face to face when I was walking with Floyd into the Kaiser Psychiatric ward for an "evaluation." On the sidewalk outside he turned to say something to me, but it wasn't Floyd at all. His eyes had shrunk into his head, almost like tiny blue beads, his mouth was contorted, his face twisted. Did the Lord allow it to manifest itself to let me know the miserable truth?

He believed that Jesus hadn't saved the world, but that he, Floyd Svensson, was the one designated to do so -- more practically, of course. One practical idea hatched in a pretty funny way when it happened.

I got a call from the Sheraton Hotel in Concord.

"Is this Mrs. Svensson?"

"Yes, this is she." I held my breath for what might be coming.

"We are working on Mr. Svensson's banquet reservation for tomorrow night. One hundred guests, is it? Can you give me more details? He hasn't gotten back to us..."

He had explained his idea to David and me, but I was unaware that he was putting it to action Supposedly he had written to 100 top scientists, physicists, and important professors, inviting them to a banquet to enlist their aid in splitting the continent of Africa. The plan was to collect all the atomic bombs in existence and to explode them in the Sahara desert. Thereby two continents would be formed, the Atlantic Ocean would join the Indian Ocean, and thus many problems would be solved, such as: shipping would be much more efficient and there would be no more water shortages in Africa -- to say nothing of ridding the world, once and for all, of atomic bombs!

I apologized to the hotel manager that the plans were off. I'm not surprised that he wasn't very gracious about it.

One day I asked his doctor to tell me on a scale of one to ten where Floyd ranked compared to his other patients. Without hesitation he groaned, "Oh, he is by far the WORST patient I've ever had!"

Amazing Love

After a particularly hard day, after bringing Floyd home from one of his lock-downs, he wanted to talk. David and I were headed for bed but he insisted on one of his family conferences. Never once had he repudiated any of his schemes; they were always alive and active, reverberating through his head. That night I was dreading another one. Maybe I even hoped that this night would bring apology or repentance – I don't know what I hoped; I was just so tired of it all.

I prayed silently, Lord, help me!

As Floyd launched forth on one of his declarations of being savior of the world, and as I looked at his too-bright eyes, suddenly my heart ached for him. I was overwhelmed with amazing love for the poor guy. There I sat wishing I was sound asleep, while the devil was tearing that man to pieces. The love I felt for him was far beyond my own ability or puny understanding – it was pure, compassionate, genuine and holy. It was Jesus' love, there is no other explanation.

Tears began to sting my eyes. I am sure I couldn't have said a word without crying. I lost track of what Floyd was exclaiming about, I just sat looking at him with incomprehensible love.

I thought, "O, thank you, Lord! Thanks. Thanks for showing me Your love for him. You know all about this crazy husband of mine, and You can take care of him when no one else can. I know that David and I will be okay too." Finally I sighed and said I'd see him in the morning. David yawned and said, "Okay, goodnight, Dad."

Floyd moved out of his chair, said goodnight to us, and turned on the TV.

My Fault Too

For years I had learned to not rock the boat. But as so often happens in my life, the Lord brought a good friend. This time it was Lois Anderson, a fellow real estate agent who was a recovered alcoholic: wise, funny, loyal and true--even my best friend till now.

During my worst months of coping we had breakfast together and prayed every morning before going to work. Lois advised me to read *The Big Book* used by Alcoholics Anonymous, and suggested I go to Alanon, which was for families of alcoholics. There I learned that I was *co-dependent*.

The book's definition: "Codependence is a tendency to behave in ways that negatively impact one's relationships and quality of life. This behavior may be characterized by denial, low self-esteem, compliance, and/or control patterns." It meant I was always adjusting my behavior to accommodate someone else's unpredictable irrationality!

There it was; it perfectly described my misguided "good girl" mentality. And in the first years of being a Christian my doing everything to keep the peace, and so forth, was reinforced by my misunderstanding *submission*.

At a very significant Alanon meeting the facilitator was telling her story: "I started coming to meetings like this twenty years ago, and early on someone leaned across the table, shook his finger at me and said, 'How long are you going to let a sick man steer your boat?'" At that she shook <u>her</u> finger at <u>me</u>.

"If nothing changes, nothing changes." They talked about the need to "create a crisis" in order to make a change. Well, there had been plenty of crises already. What now?

The lights went on –finally! --and I began to understand that I had choices. My thinking changed. I'd been struggling to survive in a smashed life boat – trying to hold on to some kind of rope ladder! All sorts of images could describe the wreckage. But it didn't need to be that way anymore. I could even jump ship, if need be, and eventually I did.

<u>The Rose Bush is Gone</u>

One night, running through Pacheco, Floyd spied a house for sale that he thought we could afford. I agreed to buy it, and sold my share of the Better Homes Orinda office to the other brokers in order to make the down payment. Thus we were back in Pacheco only a few blocks from where we had started 31 years ago.

It was some comfort to Floyd that we owned our own house, especially as it was on a double lot, a little house in front, and a legal sized lot in back. The possibilities filled him with ideas of moving another house back there.

Then tragedy had struck: only ten days after we moved there Nora and Lauren were killed. The ownership of a house was irrelevant to coping with sorrow.

As the days went by, I took comfort in a rambling old rose bush full of pink blossoms. I thought of it as a sturdy old lady watching over the driveway. She had her own exuberance, blooming faithfully, spreading sweet fragrance like a kind hand reaching out to me. She gave me hope and reminded me that God is real and all things He does are beautiful.

But Floyd was soon his restless self: he just HAD to move a house to the back lot. He showed me the house he wanted to move and begged me, with tears in his eyes, to approve. I finally caved in, and a few days later drove with a friend to see Jonni in Blaine.

When I got home two weeks later, the shabby house was sitting back there, waiting to be restored. And when I saw it, all hope for normalcy changed to dread, or --maybe that <u>was</u> normalcy.

Then I realized, "The rose bush is gone!" Obviously there had been no effort to save it in the path of a house coming through the driveway.

I went into the living room and there was Floyd lying on the couch watching TV. Looking at him, suddenly I lost heart. Anything I had left for him drained out of me like spaghetti coming out of my toes. I had absolutely nothing else to give and nothing at all to say. I was completely empty.

I just turned around, left the house, drove away and didn't go back.

Oh, God! Am I just an old rose bush in the way of a moving house?

PART FOUR

Pressing On

Brethren, I do not count myself to have apprehended; but one thing I do, forgetting those things which are behind, and reaching toward those things which are ahead, I press toward the prize for the upward call of God in Christ Jesus.
[Philippians 3:13-14]

Wells Fargo Recovery

In 1984, the year after Nora died, I started working for Wells Fargo Bank: Real Estate Recovery Officer, a fancy name for handling foreclosed homes. I never missed the irony of answering the phone, "Wells Fargo -- Recovery!" If they had known the state of my head and how much recovery I needed, they might never have hired me!

The job required a lot of me and I began to regain my balance, because in the previous three years I had run away from home six different times and been on such an emotional roller coaster... well, you know about that by now.

In the Recovery department there were only four officers at the time I joined the bank. On my first day my supervisor handed me close to fifty pink message slips that needed to be answered. Some of them were weeks old because nobody had time to respond.

Being the only Realtor on active duty, I caught on quickly. If the property was occupied after the legal time limit, a sheriff's eviction might be needed. Once in the Bank's possession, the property had to be inspected, appraised, repaired if necessary, and put on the market for resale. Coming to the bank with over twenty years of real estate experience, this was a great job for me, and the Lord's provision.

It wasn't long before I was making trips all over California on recovery assignments. Most situations were routine, some sad, and a few potentially dangerous and might require a private security guard to accompany me in case an angry owner showed up violent.

I would fly to the closest airport, rent a car, and head for the appointed agent's office, or to the property. If an eviction was needed I met at the property with a deputy sheriff, a moving van, and the guard who stayed with me through the whole procedure, packing the moving van, etc.

The officers went first and told any occupant it was time to leave. When they were gone, it was up to me to see that everything was itemized carefully – the Bank wanted no liability when – or if – the owners came to pay the storage bill and reclaim their stuff.

In one situation when the deputies entered the house, which seemed deserted, they discovered a grandmother and two young women cowering in a closet -- three frightened women dressed in colorful Indian saris. I wanted to go and comfort them, but could only watch as the deputies gently led them to the police car and drove them away. They weren't being arrested, just taken to headquarters till someone could come and get them. I felt sorry for them; I don't know if they even understood English.

"God be with them!" I prayed.

General's Dog Dish

A certain tract of expensive homes in Riverside backed up to a casino on an Indian reservation. The home owners were fed up because all night and all day the giant ventilators belched tobacco smoke and other gasses, poisoning the air, and a steady stream of chartered bus loads of gamblers churned by spewing exhaust fumes.

The house which I was to repossess was not ten feet from the back wall of the casino. I wondered if the owner had simply walked away in discouragement.

There was a security gate at the bottom of his driveway, which was the first lock to pick. An enormous brown dog bounded out to welcome us, not suspecting he'd be carted off to the pound as soon as animal control arrived -- and did so very kindly.

It was a gracious two story home with a curved staircase up to a balcony on the second floor, exuding class and good taste. The sheriff's deputy confirmed there was no one home and left. The guard relaxed, the two movers positioned the van by the front door, and the job began.

While I was busy inside later on, the gate buzzer buzzed and I went down the driveway to see who was there. It was the owner looking very worried outside the gate.

"I'm Stanley. I know I can't come in," he said sadly, "but would you mind bringing General's dog dish out?"

I didn't mind; I knew just where his super big dish was waiting to be packed. I fetched it for him, the dog food too, and handed them over the gate. Poor guy, I thought, can't go back in his own house, but I'm glad he's got General to keep him company.

Stanley's was the most immaculate home I'd run across. It was absolutely spotless, furnished with expensive antiques of all kinds – even a massive old barber's chair with bright red upholstery, gleaming and grand, looking at itself in a six-foot gold framed mirror — almost like a throne room.

There was not a single magazine, newspaper, or a letter lying around, or even a book anywhere. But I did find a book in the coffee table drawer, one I recognized, by a Jewish hippie who had become a Christian. I wondered if he'd read it.

I came across an old fashioned round top trunk. Knowing I needed to inventory everything, I opened it -- and stopped cold! Before I touched a thing I called the three men in the house. "Come and witness, this," I said, "I don't want anybody making up a story about this and I want you to watch what I do." We all looked in astonishment at hundreds of coins, sets of them, boxes of them, loose coins of all sorts and sizes. It was almost as good as a movie where the hero stumbles across a pirate's chest overflowing with gold! It was almost as good as a movie where the hero

Some things take quick thinking, and I thought quick. While two of the guys stared, I sent the other for the strongest packing box he had. Then I carefully emptied the trunk, batch by batch, and put everything in the box without trying to make an inventory as I was supposed to do. I taped it shut with lots of tape, then took a black felt marker and drew circles all around, on and off the tape and on the cardboard, so that if anybody tampered with it we would definitely know.

I phoned my boss and asked him what to do. This is far too valuable to take to storage; can I take it to a branch here and lock it up in the vault? Yes, he agreed.

I called Judy, the agent assigned to this foreclosure. "Come over here we gotta job to do!" As soon as the movers left, the guard loaded the coins into her ritzy Karmann Ghia, I locked up Stanley's place, we found Riverside Wells Fargo and unloaded the pirate's cash into their vault. The next day when I was back at Stanley's house finishing up, a lady at the branch called to tell me they didn't have room for the coins and I'd have to take them to the San Bernardino branch.

I rounded up Judy again and when we got to the bank we were told that we couldn't put the box in her car. Since the Bank was now responsible for its safety, we'd have to have a bank employee take it.

An unimpressive bank guard, gun in belt, came around with his pickup, loaded the coins in the truck bed; and we took off; me in the passenger seat, Judy in her car following right behind.

I struck up a conversation: "Do you like your job?"
"Yep, it's the first job I've had in a while."
"How long have you been working for the bank?"
"Oh, about two weeks, I guess."

94

This didn't make me feel very confident – with thousands of dollars of coins out there in the truck bed. Who was this inexperienced fellow?

In the meantime I'm looking at his gun and looking out the window, and noted that we are on some old dirt road passing a gravel pit -- to who knows where!

I began to pray, "Lord, I might be in trouble."

"Are you sure you know the way to San Bernardino?"

"Oh, yeah. I go there all the time."

"Lord, I'm pretty sure we're in trouble! Please take care of me – and Judy too." I thought we might be shot or robbed or left for dead in this gravel pit – or worse.

Finally the guy made a few turns, we came out on a real street and eventually got to the bank where I personally walked into the vault and witnessed the coin collection safely put away.

Judy let out a long breath. "Whew! When I saw that gravel pit I knew we were lost. I began praying like crazy. I thought I might have to run him off the road, knock him out with my tire iron or something, and rescue you!"

In my office several weeks later my phone rang: "This is San Bernardino: We have a man here who wants the coin collection we're holding, but he has no identification except a racquetball club membership card."

Quick, think, Becky. I wouldn't recognize Stanley if I saw him, much less remember his voice. How can I identify him over the phone? [Help, God!]

"Put him on the phone," I said. I had an idea.

"Is this Mr. Stanley?"

"Yes, ma'am."

"Tell me, Mr. Stanley, when was the last time you spoke to me?"

"Well, I guess when you gave me back General's dog dish." "Okay, give the phone back to the bank lady."

"It's okay," I told her, "give Mr. Stanley his coins. It's the right guy."

Stanley had wasted no time rescuing his beloved pooch from the pound. Perhaps General was the only love in his immaculate life. Everything else, house, antiques, coins, was cold comfort.

Thanks, God, for dogs.

Precious in the Sight of the Lord

>   Precious in the sight of the Lord
>   Is the death of His godly ones.
>   [Psalm 116:15]

I had rented an apartment in Walnut Creek with a sliding glass door to a private little yard. It was a peaceful haven for me, provided by the mercy of God. Floyd was making do in the moved-in house or in his car; I had filed for a legal separation and rarely saw him. I was busy on my job with Wells Fargo and doing okay.

The family had dealt with my leaving him, on various levels of acceptance, but Janie was pretty upset. At one point she said, "I don't see why you just don't shoot each other and be done with it!"

I understood her feelings, but didn't try to justify my reasons.

On Easter Sunday, April 6, 1986, Eric and Marlene invited the family for dinner. Floyd was there and we talked quite civilly, which ended in our driving together to the top of Mt. Diablo that evening. When the ride was over, my heart was touched by his loneliness, and I invited him to come home to my apartment.

It didn't seem all that risky, and I was soon to find out that it was exactly what the Lord wanted – that he be with the family for what was ahead.

On Wednesday that week I drove up to check out a house in Eureka, way up the coast, and came home quite late. About nine thirty when I was nearly asleep, Janie phoned me. "Mom," she said, "please pray for me. I'm having trouble breathing."

It is always a privilege when the kids ask for prayer, so of course I prayed, and then went to sleep. I had no idea that it would be the last time I heard her voice.

The next morning at work Marlene called to tell me Janie was in the hospital – in a fourth stage coma! I didn't know how serious that was, but left the office immediately and drove to the Antioch hospital. Alan had taken the kids to a baby sitter because she'd made a doctor's appointment for later that morning. But she didn't make it; she called 911. When the medics got there she was waiting for them on the front walk of her house, lying with her head on a pillow, not breathing.

They got her breathing on a resuscitator, but then her heart stopped. Frantically -- and I should say, by God's grace--

they got her heart beating, but she never breathed again on her own.

At first the doctors were puzzled: was it a bee sting, an allergic reaction to something? What, they didn't know at first. The final conclusion was viral pneumonia, which we learned is so critical that even if diagnosed quickly many patients die, as before they catch it their lungs fill with fluid and they literally drown. The clues we'd overlooked were a gurgling sound and difficulty breathing.

Eric knew what a fourth stage coma meant but I didn't till I arrived and found him sobbing in the ICU. Janie was brain dead! He and Janie had a special bond not only in their faith but in their goofy sense of humor. They would laugh together over something I would never quite catch on to. What great friends they were.

The Svenssons gathered again: another tragedy! But this time, not only the family gathered but hundreds of others. They were an amazing testimony to Janie's love for Jesus, which had touched countless lives, especially Afghan refugees. God surely must have supernaturally enabled her to speak Farsi so quickly in her first three months in Kabul.

The ICU nurses estimated that five hundred people had come to pay their last respects, even entire Afghan families she had helped; she was their beloved friend and benefactor.

All day long the waiting room was crowded — a waitress, a mail carrier, a teacher, her best friends, her church family, strangers to each other sharing their stories of how Janie was their friend; how much they owed her. Alan brought a notebook after the second day in which her friends wrote tributes to her.

The hospital staff was unaccountably kind to allow all these people to pack the waiting room and to crowd in and honor her. God bless 'em.

By California law, in a case where there is "no hope" or "brain death" the assigned doctor must, within 24 hours, inform the patient's family of their option to donate organs and / or disconnect life support.

he doctor was a compassionate guy; I doubt he wanted to have that meeting, but was understanding and matter of fact. He told us that if we didn't let them transplant Janie's heart soon, it would be too damaged to be useful. The nurse, standing by with her arms folded, nodded her head. I suddenly saw a picture of their wheeling Janie into an operating room and taking out her heart –horrors!

The next day Alan gave me a handwritten 3x5 card, one of many he handed out. I still have it my Bible and transcribe it here:

"I believe God is going to do something today.

I'd like people to pray and fast the rest of the day. Pray that God will make His Specific Will known to me and give me the faith and obedience to follow it."

God answered Alan's prayer: It wasn't the time; she wasn't to be "harvested" as they called it. Alan told us that he didn't want to explain someday to Jonathan and Anna that he had decided when she should die; her life was in God's hands, not his, no matter what other choices there were.

I saw God's mercy in this because we had time to say goodbye. If she had gone as suddenly and horribly as Nora had, I know I would have had almost too much to bear. As it was, God gave me time to reach the kind of peace He gives -- peace that surpasses understanding.

Janie's own absolute trust in Jesus nourished me. Even though she showed not the slightest sign of life, lying there with machines all around, I spent every possible hour talking to her, holding her hand, and praying.

At the hospital every time I walked down the black and white tiled corridors, I put one foot in each square like a marching soldier: "I walk in faith and victory, I walk in faith and victory, for the Lord my God is with me; I walk in faith and victory..." till I got to her bed in the ICU.

She'd been in a coma for two weeks when the call came: "Janie's heart has just slowed down and stopped." Floyd and I hurried over to the quiet room where Alan was sitting beside her. I hugged Alan, then I lifted up Janie's hand, which was still a little warm, and told her good-bye.

I'd already shed so many tears ... Well, God, this is really goodbye. Thank you for Janie, thank you for all she's meant to me and to us all. I know you love her. Lord, I'm going to miss her SO much!

We drove home without saying anything—how many silent trips like that had we had already! I don't know what Floyd felt or thought. It was too much to talk about. Janie had gone to heaven where she would see Jesus face to face.

God, your ways are not our ways, are they?

Epilogue

Gloria Jane Ichikawa: June 4, 1952 - April 24. 1986.
She was 33 years old and left behind Alan who had to be dad and mom for Jonathan, going on five, and Anna who turned three when Janie was in the hospital.

Floyd stayed with me three weeks or so. He was subdued and sad at first, then that old demon showed up again and led him on a wild escapade to Los Angeles and back, some sort of convention where he bought a bunch of expensive books and other stuff on my credit card.

I told him I couldn't go back to all that craziness all over again -- I was out of the boat and he was on his own. I was not responsible for him; he would have to move along -- which he did.

I knew that God had connected him back with me and the family for a time so that he wouldn't face the crisis while living in his car, drying his socks and underwear on the side view mirrors. Hard as it was, Mom would have called the interlude one of those "Pretty ways of Providence."

The Ex- Police Officer

My leaving Floyd occurred about a year and a half after I started working for Wells Fargo. Sometimes he would come to the office for something or other, but I didn't really want to see him. One day, though, another person came asking for me, a man about forty, looking very troubled, twisting a baseball hat in his hands.

Not knowing whether he was bringing bad news about Floyd, or what, I excused myself from the office and went out to his car.

"Mrs. Svensson," he apologized, "please forgive me for interrupting you, but I just have to talk to you -- would you sit in my car for a few minutes?"

Of course I couldn't refuse, so I sat in the passenger seat. He draped his arms over the steering wheel --

"I have to tell you ... I was one of the officers who responded to the 911 call when your daughter and granddaughter were murdered."

I did a quick calculation, "That was over two years ago."

"Yes, Ma'am, I know. But I just can't get over it. I am a Viet Nam vet and I never saw anything as bad as that all the time I was in 'Nam."

My heart began to pound, what could I say? "Thank you for coming to see me. What is your name?"

"Williams, Ma'am; Joe Williams. And I've quit the police force. I had to go on leave to get counseling, but it didn't help. I still see the picture of that little girl ..... and..." he buried his face in his hands and sobbed.

I shifted in the seat and put my arm around his shoulder. "Joe, I don't know what to say. But it's okay to cry..."

"Thanks for talking to me. I...just don't know what to do..."

"Joe, sometimes you just have to talk to somebody," I said, remembering how it had been for me; sometimes the only thing that helped was if somebody would listen.

Sniffing and rubbing his nose with the back of his hand, Joe said, 'But it's been such a long time..."

"I know, Joe. People will tell you to get over it, but it's not time... the bad stuff doesn't go away by itself."

He sucked in his breath and tried to speak more calmly. 'Yeah, but what do I do?"

"Joe, believe me. I wouldn't be here talking to you today if Jesus hadn't helped me through all this. Are you a Christian, Joe?"

"I don't know. I think so."

"Joe, I used to think I had all the answers and I could be a good person if I tried hard enough, but I didn't know that God wants me to depend on Him, not on myself."

"Well, I don't know much about that."

"I can't comfort you, but Jesus can. He sends his Holy Spirit. I didn't know anything about the Holy Spirit for a long time, but then I found out that He is the Comforter."

"Huh. How do you mean?"

"Well, when you become a Christian the Holy Spirit kind of takes over. That's what Jesus meant when He said the Comforter would be in us."

"I guess I need to know more about this because I sure as heck aren't getting any comfort these days."

Then I asked Joe if I could pray for him and he agreed.

"Lord Jesus, please comfort Joe. Show him who you are and heal all those terrible memories and wipe those awful pictures away. Give him peace, Lord. I know you love him..."

Then I told him about Fair Oaks Church which was just a few blocks away, and invited him to check it out.

I realized I'd been away from the office quite a long time and that from then on Joe was in God's hands. So we got out of the car, and Joe came around to shake my hand. But instead I hugged him.

"Thanks for coming, Joe..." then I suddenly thought to ask, "Were you one of the men who rushed Lauren to the hospital?"

"Yes, Ma'am, I was. She was...so...so...bad ... I just can't talk about it.." then he almost started to cry again.

"Oh, Joe. I'm so sorry. I'm so sorry. But you did everything you could. Nothing could have saved her; the doctors told us so. But thank you for being a hero that day. I know you'll be okay, and I'll keep praying for you."

Some days are like that. You never know when the Holy Spirit will show up and give you a chance to tell somebody how He has helped you through things. Folks are fond of saying that well, God never gives you more than you can handle. And I say, wrong! God absolutely gives you more than you can handle so that you <u>have</u> to turn it all over and depend on him!

PART FIVE

Starting Over

I will lift up my eyes to the mountains
From whence shall my help come?
My help comes from the LORD
Who made heaven and earth.
He will not allow your foot to slip;
He who keeps you will not slumber.
Behold, He who keeps Israel
Will neither slumber nor sleep.
The LORD is your keeper;
The LORD is your shade on your right hand.
The sun will not smite you by day,
Nor the moon by night.
The LORD will protect you from all evil;
He will keep your soul.
The LORD will guard your going out and
    your coming in
From this day forth and even forever.

[Psalm 121]

Starting Over

In 1988 my 41 year marriage was over; Floyd was remarried and my job was switched — due to some inner politics — from Real Estate Recovery to foreclosing on auto loans, which was total confusion: no instruction, no experience, no personal contact; just looking at numbers on a computer screen.

I lost my hearing and spent a month of being completely deaf, <u>and</u> was seeing double. Five different doctors said I couldn't possibly see double out of only one eye (the other never did focus) and one said to cheer up -- it was only stress. Finally I lost my taste. That was such a bummer I didn't even mention it to anyone. I even wondered whether I should check myself into a hospital. I just plugged along, but Jonni was aware of my struggles and was worried about me.

On my scheduled vacation in August I flew to Seattle. Jonni met my plane with a plan to go thru the mountains for a couple of days before going home to Ferndale. After that pleasant trip when we got back to Bellingham she took me to Anthony's, a fine restaurant on the harbor, where she ordered special hors d'oeuvres, special sea food, and a bottle of wine. After comfortably settling down, she looked me in the eye and said, "Mom, we really want you to come and live with us."

It had to have been one of the most precious minutes of my life, that my daughter and her family would extend that kind of love to me. I couldn't remember anything ever like it. I'm sure I was crying, or about to, when I accepted.

I returned to California, resigned from Wells Fargo, sold the condo I had bought, arranged to move my stuff, and two months later Jonni came down to drive me to Ferndale. I was leaving Janie's little kids behind, Eric and his family, my church, everything I'd known for 36 years in the Bay Area, but I couldn't look back. Even though I might be losing a close relationship with my grandchildren, I was too near drowning to refuse the life preserver Jonni had thrown out to me.

Jonni and Bob, besides welcoming me, cut a huge picture window in the spare bedroom so I could look out on Mt. Baker. And their favorite optometrist examined my eyes and said that sometimes a contact lens would solve double vision – which it did, thank the Lord! What a boost that was to my morale right off the bat.

For the next two years I unwound. At first I couldn't sleep and played solitaire with miniature cards, sitting up in bed till I got so tired they fell out of my hands. I joined a tennis club and played tennis three or four times a week, banging away, till I finally relaxed enough to sell my membership and move on.

Thanks to people who prayed for me, and thanks for God's amazing grace, I gradually began to feel that He still had something ahead for me – and maybe even yet, for Him.

Whatcom Pregnancy Center

Jonni and a group of friends had a burden to start a crisis pregnancy center in Bellingham to serve the women of Whatcom County. I was in on the beginning in a mild way, able to help a little bit. In the process my eyes were opened to the terrible evil of abortion, which I had not really thought much about till then.

As I listened to impassioned hearts of Pro-Lifers I realized that I was guilty! I was guilty of taking life every bit as much as a young misguided girl going to an abortion clinic.

I remembered back at Sleepy Hollow in the early seventies, Patty, who we had invited to live with us, who had been on welfare in Tacoma. She'd been with us a few weeks when it turned out she was pregnant.

I had lost no time in hustling her back to Washington to do away with "it!" It seemed the right option for her because she had been at a party where several boys in one night all had sex with her. I had neither the wisdom nor the compassion to deal with her any other way, and also thought I was somehow protecting Nora, who was twelve. Oh, God, forgive me!

How logic does unravel in retrospect!

But besides that, I realized that in my eagerness to have my tubes tied after David was born – six is enough! – I had caused an ectopic pregnancy that had to be ended surgically. I was not a Christian yet, I didn't have the backing of anyone who encouraged big families; all I wanted was to not be so busy with kids!

Nobody to blame but my own selfishness -- I even joked about the messenger who was not deterred by rains, sleet, wind or snow -- that precious little life destroyed.

With the Whatcom Pregnancy Center coming to life around me, I was convicted and ashamed of my hard-headedness. I asked God to forgive me for causing that little baby to die. I had been in such a hurry to be on with my life that I never asked the doctor a simple question: was it a boy or a girl? But then, 25 years later, I knew I would have had a little brother for David, and I would have named him Robert

Eugene after the two Morse brothers I had met in Calcutta; his middle name would have been the same as Dad's and Floyd's – and mine.

Oh, my! Going through the guilt for Patty, and my own loss, how much compassion I feel now for thousands -- millions!-- of could-have-been moms who grieve for their babies years and years after. God have mercy on us all!

I'm so grateful God says to me and to every one of them, "If we confess our sins He is faithful and just to forgive us our sins and cleanse us from all unrighteousness." [1 John 1:9] Where would I –any of us -- be without His forgiveness, and what guilt and misery would I have experienced otherwise.

Christ for the Nations

In the summer of 1991 I helped man a pro-life booth in the Lynden Fair. On a break while wandering around other booths I came across Christ for the Nations Bible College where Sue and Gerald Nussbaum were passing out free cups of water. We got to sharing experiences and I decided to visit the college in Surrey just across the border. Next thing I knew, I had enrolled in CFN Canada! I was already a great grandmother, but I kept the great part quiet – enough that I was enrolled, the oldest student, Grandma Becky, age 65.

The Nussbaums became wonderful friends. They were in their thirties and full of enthusiasm. Sue had naturally dark red hair that fell to her waist, and Gerald was tall, fun, and competent. They had been high school sweethearts and worked together like clockwork. It was they who led the outreach team that helped me find our old school and house in Shanghai.

Before classes had started I met Richard and Jose, two young men who also were headed for CFN. Richard had driven from Massachusetts with his three kids and pregnant wife, all his possessions inside and on top of an old station wagon, and so sure he was intended for Bible college that he didn't even mail his application till he was half way across the country.

Jose was fresh out of the army where he had become a Christian in Korea, and was now bent on going to Mexico to evangelize kids like himself.

The three of us carpooled across the border; Jose and I started from Ferndale and picked up Richard in Birch Bay. Jose and I would time Richard when he got in the car: how long till he would rub his hands together and burst out with some exclamation, such as, "I can't believe that guy at work; I have been praying for him THREE WHOLE DAYS and he FINALY accepted the Lord!" Or "Praise the Lord! You won't believe what happened to me...." and regale us with his latest happy miracle.

We gobbled up school like hungry puppies. Each trip we shared what we'd learned, Jose and Richard overflowing with enthusiasm for what God was doing. On some days our rides back and forth were worth as much as the classes themselves.

Free Indeed

Therefore, if the Son sets you free, you shall be free indeed.   [John 8:36]

Jesus said He came to set the captives free --even when they don't know they are captives. Most likely, the most significant setting free in my life came at the end of my first year at Bible college.

Each semester closed with a special worship and prayer service. Before leaving we divided into small groups with a faculty member to pray for each of us. When it was my turn to be prayed for, I took a deep breath because I was reluctant to tell the group the embarrassing problem that had plagued me for years.

"I have a problem," I hesitated. Then I decided to go for it: "You see, whenever I am with men in a group praying, or even when listening to a preacher I see their sexual parts floating across my vision. I just can't shake it off, no matter what; I'm ashamed, and I hate this thing!"

Immediately Mr. B and a pastor's wife in the group stood up and put their hands on my head. "Lord God," Mr. B. prayed, "you know Becky didn't invite this stuff into her head. I command it to leave in the name of Jesus Christ and NEVER come back!"

Then all of them prayed, even more fervently, rebuking the devil and asking God to cleanse me. Suddenly my head felt as though Alka -Seltzer was sizzling through my head; I could virtually hear something swooshing out; I was a little shaky and amazed.

Gaining my equilibrium, I said, "I believe and accept in the name of Jesus that this thing is gone and will never come back. Thank you, Lord, thank you, thank you!"

Home alone that night, still thanking God, I asked, "What was that, what has happened, Lord?"

"Well, my child," I heard. 'You have not only been set free from the image that wouldn't leave you alone, but you have been set free from *the ancient Chinese female rejection* that was put on you when you were born!"

Goodness, I'd never heard of such a thing. How, Lord? Who did it and why? How did it happen to me?

Well, that's the way it is in China. Passed on by the nurses, the servants around me, even by the doctor who delivered me in a culture where girl babies were thrown out to die or simply neglected and devalued. They may not be aware they are passing on a curse to a baby because it has been so deeply ingrained in their attitudes and subconsiousness for centuries.

This was such a big revelation I could hardly process it.

The next thing I realized was freedom from an ugly thing that had been like a huge dead uprooted tree stump, with dirt dripping off its roots, blocking my way in the middle of my house –something that I had walked around and had to avoid every step of my whole life.

It was inferiority to men –any man. I had even felt subservient to my own sons, to say nothing of my father, brothers, husband, teachers –every male person in my life!

I had to learn to "walk" a new way. That roadblock wasn't there anymore; I could walk straight ahead because there was no longer anything to avoid. I didn't have to be the good little girl who was afraid to speak up or was less valuable than a boy or a man; nor to compare myself to them or put myself down. I had value just as I am.

I felt as free as a gifted pianist must feel when he can let his fingers fly over the keys with absolute abandon. I never again had that ugly presence forcing its way into my thoughts, and today I have as many good men friends as women. Hallelujah!

On an outreach trip to Malaysia I shared this release with three Chinese women in a Bible study. Their eyes lit up with wonder -- and tears-- when they realized they too had been suffering from female rejection. Each one had a story: one had been given away when she was little because her parents wanted a boy; one said she believed this would transform her marriage because she had always been in angry competition with her husband. She prayed that she could relax and let him be the leader of her house.

Smuggling Bibles

Bible smuggling? Of course, what else do you do when you have run out of other adventures? I didn't really expect to, but I caught the fever after my first trip back to China in 1993. It was so wonderful just to be back where I felt so much at home. And besides that, China is beautiful, the people are friendly, and the Christians are a joyful bunch.

The operation, "Donkeys for Jesus," was organized by Revival Chinese Ministries in Hong Kong, which a Viet Nam vet, Dennis Balcolm started with no money and no backing; nothing but a big heart for China. Now he is known world-wide and gets much credit for supporting the house church [underground] movement throughout China.

Our day started from housing provided by the ministry, then walking or going by bus to their headquarters where we loaded up with Bibles. I wrapped a heavy canvas-like apron around my waist, then packed its three rows of small pockets, each of which would hold a small vinyl covered Bible. I learned to pick which pockets to leave empty so I could sit down if I needed to, or to keep them from banging against my knees. Over that I wore a very much too big sun dress which covered me up.

On other occasions we packed Bibles in backpacks and pulled "blind bags" of clothing or even vitamins.

A different small team of people would gather for every trip and would not start out before earnest prayer that the eyes of any officials would be <u>blinded</u>! Teams were sent out about an hour apart so that they didn't arouse more suspicion than necessary.

A variety of people were recruited, anybody from kids to grandparents, the more variety the better -- tourist types -- of all nationalities rather than Asians.

We approached the border by train or bus, then spread out between the eight or ten check points and pretended we didn't know each other. We checked through customs and immigration on the Hong Kong side, then crossed a terribly stinky creek (full of sewage) to Shenzhen on the China side. There we had two more inspections, immigration and customs, before we put our bags through an airport like X-ray, picked them up and blended into the crowd till we rendezvoused again at a designated gathering spot.

If we were delivering Bibles only to Shenzhen, we took them to hiding places around the city, usually an office, where hey were kept till enough were collected to send a team on a longer trip inland.

A day trip took six or eight hours. Then another trip the next day, five or six days a week.

Going anywhere was not a simple matter of hopping into a nice private automobile with a passenger or two, but always being pushed, crowded, standing endlessly in line, or sometimes even being squashed to the point I couldn't raise my arms if I needed to. The best way to describe the crossings is to picture a mob pouring out of a football field after a game. The Chinese are just pouring out of everywhere!

Especially hard for me were not the day trips which were relatively easy, but on long overnight trips. Crowding onto an escalator that might go up two flights from ground level to the railroad track, I sometimes thought I might be trampled in the crush.

Always on the long train trips, we each dragged a big bag of Bibles – wheely bags, we called them – till we got located in the train compartment. If one of the team found a place on the train before the rest of us caught up, he could open the window and let us pass the bags up to him.

The railroad cars have an aisle on one side where six feet above our heads the guys hoisted the bags up to a rack for the trip. Amazingly, no one seemed to question what they contained.

On the other side of the car are rows of open compartments each with three bunks on each side facing each other, the highest about eight feet up there. It was a friendly arrangement, and no one complained. Hawkers came through regularly with snacks and styrofoam boxes of hot rice and boiled eggs.

Every car had a monitor who went through every few hours and collected the garbage in a black bag which he took to the last window in the car and threw out! He was also responsible to enforce the no smoking signs which everyone ignored, unless one of us would take him to task and point out his failure to enforce the rules.

A trip from Hong Kong to Shanghai took 38 hours, on the average, depending on whether there was a land slide or other complications on the way. Going to the bathroom was horrible – squatting over an open hole that dumped everything on the tracks, provided the previous visitor had aimed right.

Well, that is China. Some things haven't changed at all -- especially the poor people along the tracks waiting for the garbage bags to fly out the windows.

On our first trip when we got to Shanghai and found our way to the hiding place, it turned out to be only about three blocks from the old Christian Literature Society where Dad had worked through the 1930's.

"Grandma" doesn't have a name that anyone mentions because she is the contact for the underground church. Her apartment in the old building had special cupboards that looked like normal walls, but when the panels were opened they exposed deep spaces for hiding Bibles.

The teams took the big canvas bags we had filled in Shenzhen, and unpacked them in Grandma's cupboards. After that, she was responsible to let the house churches know when to come and pick them up. Grandma was over eighty, a dear quiet lady who sat with her hands folded together across her tummy in typical Chinese poise.

Our guide and interpreter, Susan, was a remarkable Chinese woman who spoke English, French, Filipino/Tagalog, and at least two Chinese dialects. She was very able to help me tell Grandma that my dad had worked for the *Gwang Shau Whey* (Good News Society) so near by.

Grandma's eyes lit up. "Ai-ya", she said, "I must tell you a story. And right at her elbow was a little black book. She reached for the book – a small diary – and flipped back to a date in 1953.

Susan interpreted: "One day the Holy Spirit told me to go to the [CLS] right away. I put down my chopstsicks because I was having lunch." She laughed, "Right away! So I went over there; the big building had been taken over, but there was a little store." She held our her hands to indicate about as big as her room. "I stood in the middle of the store and said, 'Now what do I do?' Then the Holy Spirit said to buy some books."

I interrupted her and asked her in Chinese, "How many?"

"Ai, hun doh!" [Very many] She stretched out her hands full wide. "'Buy some of everything!' he told me. So I bought some of all the books in the store and I had to get a taxi to help me bring them home."

Then she shook her head, "You know, the Communists came the very next day and destroyed all the books in the store and locked it up!"

"Wow! You were just in time. What did you do with them all?"

"My husband," she explained, "was making regular trips to Hong Kong back then, and he told a Christian friend who published books about the books I'd saved. His friend asked him to bring the books to Hong Kong so they could publish them again. Nothing had been printed for the Chinese churches in a long time, and from the copies I saved they started to publish them again."

I was absolutely dumbfounded. Here in this humble place, this precious old lady, was the only one of over a billion people in China who knew what happened to the Christian Literature Society after Dad had left Shanghai! Does God love making connections, or what?

Susan was so thrilled she said she couldn't be more excited if she had found herself falling out of an airplane!

"Grandma" with her worn diary up on her left.

After that, I made three more "Donkey trips." In all, I crossed the border from Hong Kong nearly a hundred times. That resulted in so many stamps in my Passport, four a day, that I needed to go to the American Consulate and get more pages added.

Only once was I intercepted – those prayer-covered eyes were really blinded! On the Hong Kong to Shenzhen crossing, if they found Bibles in our stuff, they gave us a formal scolding, took our loot away to storage and when we returned to re-enter Hong Kong, we could reclaim it by paying a storage fee – not a lot of money, and the Bibles were retreived to be delivered another day.

The wonderful thing about delivering Bibles was that each one would perhaps be handled by twenty people – a whole little church – or more! What a privilege to have been part of that ministy!

And the best part of those trips were the rare occasions when we actually met the house church believers. One night a secret meeting was arranged in a hotel room where we met a group about 12 men and women, some of them who had been in prison; some of them were pastors not even twenty years old, infectiously joyful. They all had stories to tell us, and we loved to worship and pray with them. What an inspiration they were!

I told one of the men that my dad had smuggled Bibles out of Shanghai in the 1940's. "Do you think any of those Bibles are still in existance?"

"OH, YES!" He grinned from ear to ear and held out his hands wide, just the way Grandma had expressed VERY MUCH. "Yes, yes, and there are fourteen generations of Christians in China!"

The very week Dad died we had heard that the doors of Communist China had opened just a crack, and that there were over three hundred thousand Christians in China. [By now 300 million or more.]

On March 22nd 1980, Jonni was with Dad in St. Luke's Hospital, holding his hand. She told him about the report from China, and mused that some of the Bibles he had smuggled were part of the good news. He weakly squeezed her hand.

Jonni said, "I love you, Granddad."

"Me too," he said. Those were his last words; and so he went to meet the Lord; mission accomplished. Praise the Lord!

The Bible Smuggler

Return to Route Winling

"French Town," in the 1930's, a section of the International Settlement of Shanghai, where the American School and the Community Church were located, was a beautiful haven from the squalor and devastation just a few blocks away. Except for Chinese shopkeepers and rickshaws, its quiet tree-lined streets might have been any affluent city in the world. Most of the classy apartments and large homes – out of sight behind high walls -- were occupied by foreigners. The proximity of French Town to the ravaged surrounding countryside seemed to have no effect on the daily life of French Town.

After the Japanese had destroyed the mission compound at South Gate, and there was continual fighting around the International Settlement, about Christmas time in 1937 we rented a house, #47 Route Winling, a few blocks from school. Though we had attended SAS since 1932, when I started first grade, and except for our short stay in the boys' dorm, we had never been in walking distance, nor a twenty-cent rickshaw ride away. Now all of us could walk or ride our bikes to school.

We weren't there long; war was creeping up on the US. By1940, after Dan and Warren had gone to Ohio for college, the American Consulate ordered its civilians to leave China as soon as possible, and the American School -- SAS-- was about to shut down.

Dad would have to abandon the Christian Literature Society, where he had been administrator since 1932. However, he stubbornly refused to go back to the States: we could go to West China, where he would continue distributing literature, and where Dicky and I could go to school in Chengdu.

I was fourteen and Dicky twelve when we left Shanghai in November 1940. The last few nights before we left I propped myself up in bed reading way past midnight, hurrying to finish reading *Gone with the Wind*. It was borrowed and I couldn't take it with me. Did I have a clue that *Gone with the Wind* could apply to me, or that I would ever be back to Shanghai? I could not possibly have thought that far ahead.

Yet, fifty-three years later, in 1993, I was one of six people on an Outreach team that delivered Bibles to an underground contact in Shanghai!

After we had delivered our precious cargo to the Chinese Christians, I couldn't wait to find our way to SAS, the church, and even the house on Route Winling. I had brought along an old map of Shanghai and though the street names had been changed by the Communist take-over, by comparing a new map,

I directed a patient taxi driver till I spotted the church-- and yes, there was SAS across the street!

We dismissed the taxi with a hefty tip, and advanced like explorers up the steps of the still sedate Colonial style school building. We were met by a polite guard, who nodded knowingly. Obviously I wasn't the first white haired lady to come back to her school!

It was now housing a maritime academy; over the years various occupants of the campus had replaced the playing fields, the track, quadrangle, and every available square yard of land with a hodgepodge of nondescript buildings. Gone too was the beautiful brick colonnade where I had jumped rope, hopscotched, and played stone-paper-scissors at recess.

Memories filled my head: I thought of my teachers: Miss Black, Mrs. Pio, and Mr. Cheney.

Miss Black in fifth grade wore high heels and really red lipstick; she was pretty, but she was cross a lot. Once I spent hours making a compass design and carefully painted different colors in the circles and shapes. When I brought it to school she took one quick look at my design and scolded, "Becky Jean Terry, don't you ever turn in something you didn't do by yourself!" I was so utterly crushed I didn't have the nerve to stick up for myself. I didn't much like fifth grade after that.

Mrs. Pio, short and erect with thick grey hair, had a voice she could project across a football field. My favorite assemblies where those where she read books to the whole school; and in sixth grade she taught me a lesson I never forgot.

As I went with the team down the hall toward the girls' bathroom, I suddenly remembered being caught just after I had reached under the stall door and dumped water on Anna Worth's feet. [She was a new girl who had never been to a regular school, who I thought was weird.] When I had turned around from my nasty deed, Mrs. Pio was facing me with her arms crossed. "Becky Jean Terry, what do you think you are doing! You go right straight home this very minute and bring back some dry stockings for Anna and *you apologize to her!*"

Never a contrite spirit skedaddled home any faster than Becky Jean Terry! I ducked into the house, grabbed my very best knee socks, and raced back to school. There is no question about it: I promised myself I'd be a good girl forever and ever and never EVER tease Anna again.

Mr. Cheney in seventh grade was my favorite. He was very tall and wore his horn-rimmed glasses across the top of his head until he needed them. When he slid them down on his nose and bent down to talk to me, I knew I was his favorite too.

One day Irene Steinman leaned over to ask me how to spell something. He overheard her and shook his finger at her: "Irene, I'd better warn you: never ask a Terry how to spell!" Then he pulled his glasses down, looked at us both, and winked. We giggled as he plunked his glasses back on his head and continued with the class.

As we left the school I almost hated to say goodbye and leave my memories behind all over again.

Next I had to take the team into the Church. Oh, my goodness! I couldn't believe I was really back; I was so overwhelmed with emotion I lost connection with my five faithful followers. I was all alone and began to cry as I wandered down the center aisle. There was the very pew in the middle of the left side where we always sat. I remembered how I used to play with Mom's hands, tracing her large veins with my fingers. I remembered waiting hopefully for the next hymn so I could stand up and sing instead of sitting so still.

The grand old pipe organ was still there. I wondered if anyone could make it sound the way it used to... yet I could almost hear the Doxology vibrating to the ceiling, bounding off the balcony and echoing around the stained-glass windows.

The polite pastor who was showing us around asked why I was weeping. In my rusty Chinese I explained that I had been a *shou hi-ze* (little child) here. Then realizing that this old Presbyterian church was now a government controlled "Three Self Church," I asked the team to make a circle with the pastor, and I prayed for the church. It was one of those times that the Holy Spirit takes over: "Father, bless this church, the house of the living God. Your word says it is the pillar and foundation of the truth. May this church fulfill its commission to be Your Truth for the Chinese people and don't let it be led astray by any false doctrine; keep it pure, Lord; it is Your church"

Thanking the pastor, and to continue my short walk to a long way back, I wanted to find our house -- if it was still there. So we started down the wide tree-lined sidewalk of Avenue Petain toward the street I remembered. Along the way familiar landmarks were still there – the trees were huge and shaggy, not smartly pruned as they used to be, but they were the same trees with their spotty peeling bark.

There was the apartment building where Leila Khouri lived. She was tall and quiet and had beautiful black eyes. I remembered in seventh grade when a boy shot a paper wad across the room and hit her right in her eye. I was the one Mr. Cheney asked to leave school, hold her hand, and walk home with her so she could go to the doctor.

We passed the Comprador –a snazzy specialty store that sold imported goods. I thought of the time I saw a pyramid of boxes in the window, each box trimmed in diagonals of light blue and dark blue: Kleenex? I liked the sound of the name but couldn't imagine that anybody could afford paper handkerchiefs that you would just throw away!

On the corner of Route Winling was a familiar seven story apartment house, still with its circular drive through a canopied entry, still with attendants in sharp green jackets. I remembered one day having gone home with red haired Joanne to the fifth floor. We helped ourselves to a snack then sneaked up to the roof garden. From there, looking across Zickaway Creek, only two blocks away, we saw some kind of skirmish going on -- a soldier was crawling up over the roof of a small house, aiming his gun at someone below. We never told anybody what we saw because we would have had to face a few more questions than we'd want to answer!

I led the team up Route Winling, and there on the first corner was #47! The street sign was changed to something Chinese, yet the exchange shop kitty corner across the intersection looked about the same as always.

And our house! It looked so much better than I remembered; somebody had demolished the old bamboo fence and replaced it with a white stucco wall; everything looked fresh and clean! When I pounded on the gate a grey haired man and a young round-faced woman cautiously looked us over. Their employers weren't home, but when I told them the *shau hi-ze* had come back they were all smiles and let us inside.

The yard was much better kept than it was back in those hot summers when we set our camp cots under the willow tree and Mom read Oz books or Winnie the Pooh to us. I could almost hear the cicadas again, those noisy critters that filled the trees and made it hard to hear Mom reading.

I posed for a picture on the little porch where Warny's pet monkey had opened my bird cage and eaten my canary.

I posed again by the front door where stucco had showered down the day Dicky and John Gordon -- both ten-- had fired a bullet through the upstairs bedroom wall. They had decided to see if one of the rifles Danny and Warny found on the battle field still worked!

[In 1937 and '38 after a battle had been won or lost nobody went out to clean up what was left. The Chinese were too superstitious to bury the bodies or to touch anything and the Japanese had better things to do. Danny and Warny and their friends could ride their bikes out there with nobody to bother them and would come back with Japanese gas masks, canteens, rifles and even ammunitions that were abandoned.]

I pictured the sweltering day when the cook had taken off his shirt and stretched out on his cot to take a nap by the back gate. The temptation was irresistible: I dared Dicky to drop some ice cubes on his bare chest, but he wouldn't take the dare. So I did! Our poor cook couldn't afford to quit his job - and sure put up with a lot of shenanigans!

We finally thanked the servants, who had enjoyed our visit as much as we did, and took their pictures too. They held our hands, in both of theirs, bowed and grinned and in good old Chinese style sent us off with many gracious pronouncements of peace and prosperity.

The visit wasn't complete, though, without stopping at the exchange shop where I used to linger over the glass counter; Milky Ways, Wrigley's gum, notebooks, pencils, and Kodak film, while the friendly store keeper waited patiently to see whether or not I was going to part with any of my allowance.

This white-haired lady who spoke Chinese with a perfect Shanghai dialect tickled the bystanders. Soon there was a little group laughing, touching my hands. Their smiles and delight said "Welcome Home" in many endearments and they agreed to pose with me for a picture.

Back to the Exchange Shop, 1993

"The Bund" Shanghai, China, 1932

Shanghai! The city I had loved, the crowded, dirty, beautiful, noisy, exotic city where I could chatter in Chinese as well as a native, where I knew my way around on a bike, where my family, my school and teachers, my church, my friends, and the moving events of history worked the clay of who I am: my home town.

Standing Beside Myself

Something beautiful happened by my returning to Route Winling. I had a sense of standing beside myself. A kind friend, a great grandma, looking at little Becky Jean; observing not myself but a little girl in a foreign land. She was conditioned to ignoring the sights and sounds of war: a city at times completely surrounded by fire, the screech of dive bombers, shells streaking overhead; horrible sights, even decaying bodies on the battlefield. She was caught in calamities, sudden changes, losses, and confusion, yet it seemed to her an ordinary life.

She was lonesome sometimes, naughty sometimes. She tried her best to be a good girl, but she needed hugs which rarely were part of the picture. She struggled to be noticed where boys mattered but it seemed that girls did not. She needed encouragement instead of scolding and squelching.

I suddenly had great compassion for her, someone I wanted to love: a little girl that I needed to comfort, to erase her guilty conscience, and to release her from all the criticism I had poured out on her. I could love her and forgive her instead of being ashamed of her and pushing her aside. Now I could tell her that Jesus had loved her back then and that He was there the day she turned twelve and nobody remembered to say Happy Birthday because she already had her party before school was out.

I'm sure the Lord planned the Outreach trip just for me: that precious child he had protected, watched over, and loved all her life. He is her Father, my Abba Father, and whether little Becky Jean back there in China, or Grandma Becky today, Jesus loves me.
This I know!

"The Bund" Shanghai, China, 1932

    Shanghai! The city I had loved, the crowded, dirty, beautiful, noisy, exotic city where I could chatter in Chinese as well as a native, where I knew my way around on a bike, where my family, my school and teachers, my church, my friends, and the moving events of history worked the clay of who I am: my home town.

Standing Beside Myself

Something beautiful happened by my returning to Route Winling. I had a sense of standing beside myself. A kind friend, a great grandma, looking at little Becky Jean; observing not myself but a little girl in a foreign land. She was conditioned to ignoring the sights and sounds of war: a city at times completely surrounded by fire, the screech of dive bombers, shells streaking overhead; horrible sights, even decaying bodies on the battlefield. She was caught in calamities, sudden changes, losses, and confusion, yet it seemed to her an ordinary life.

She was lonesome sometimes, naughty sometimes. She tried her best to be a good girl, but she needed hugs which rarely were part of the picture. She struggled to be noticed where boys mattered but it seemed that girls did not. She needed encouragement instead of scolding and squelching.

I suddenly had great compassion for her, someone I wanted to love: a little girl that I needed to comfort, to erase her guilty conscience, and to release her from all the criticism I had poured out on her. I could love her and forgive her instead of being ashamed of her and pushing her aside. Now I could tell her that Jesus had loved her back then and that He was there the day she turned twelve and nobody remembered to say Happy Birthday because she already had her party before school was out.

I'm sure the Lord planned the Outreach trip just for me: that precious child he had protected, watched over, and loved all her life. He is her Father, my Abba Father, and whether little Becky Jean back there in China, or Grandma Becky today, Jesus loves me.

This I know!

The Dream

In April, 2007, after Floyd had been in a nursing home for awhile, he was suddenly hospitalized because it appeared he was dying. All of us gathered together at Eric and Marlene's house, their being the closest to the hospital, to bid him farewell.

However, it wasn't his time to die. On a quiet morning Grace went alone to the hospital, and through a tender conversation, mutual forgiveness, and prayer, Floyd asked Jesus to forgive his sins, and accepted Him as his Savior.

Oh, there was great rejoicing in the Svensson family – and more so in heaven. The crazy, goofy, old guy was a new creature in Christ and his last two years were peaceful. Hallelujah!

.He was 87 when he died on June 23rd, 2009. His wife, Marina, his kids, and some of his grandsons were there to say goodbye.

Not long ago God gave me a dream:
I was entering from a side room into an elegant ballroom. The floor was laid with large black and white marble tiles that gleamed in the twilight coming through tall windows on my right. I had a cleaning rag in my hands.

Across the room on the far left, another door opened and Floyd came in. He looked like he used to look, and he also was carrying a cloth of some kind in his hand. I dropped my rag, and approached him as he dropped his.

As I walked toward him, I held out my arms in a dancing position and asked him to dance. He slowly took me in his arms and a little awkwardly began to dance. I tried to hum a tune which didn't exactly work, and he said not to bother.

Suddenly the place was filled with music: a grand swelling symphony orchestra playing a majestic old hymn. What was it? Then I recognized *"Love Divine, All loves excelling; Joy of heaven to earth come down"* reverberating all through the room as though coming straight from heaven. Our dancing came together in perfect harmony as we swirled around and around the elegant room.

It was so dear, so sweet; the abundance of Jesus' own love pouring over us -- restoring our love and the joy in each other we once had.

I believe God lifted me up for a glimpse into the sweetness of eternity. All my memories, all pain, every loss was

restored by Jesus' all consuming love; truly the joy of heaven to earth come down!
    O thank You, Lord, for a beautiful ending to the story.

Love Divine

Love divine, all loves excelling,
Joy of heaven to earth come down,
Fix in us Thy humble dwelling,
All Thy faithful mercies crown.
Jesus, Thou are all compassion,
Pure, unbounded love Thou art,
Visit us with Thy salvation;
Enter every trembling heart.

Breath, O breathe, Thy loving Spirit
Into every troubled breast!
Let us all in Thee inherit,
Let us find thy second rest.
Take away our bent to sinning,
Alpha and Omega be;
End of faith, as its beginning,
Set our hearts at liberty.

Come, almighty to deliver,
Let us all Thy life receive;
Suddenly return, and never,
Nevermore Thy temples leave:
There we would be always blessing,
Serve Thee as Thy hosts above,
Pray, and praise Thee without ceasing,
Glory in Thy perfect love.

Finish then Thy new creation,
Pure and spotless let us be;
Let us see Thy great salvation
Perfectly restored in Thee:
Change from glory into glory,
Till in heaven we take our place,
Till we cast our crowns before Thee,
Lost in wonder, love, and praise.

[Charles Wesley, 1701-1788]

Made in the USA
Charleston, SC
18 November 2013